Arthur Erickson Critical Works

NICHOLAS OLSBERG AND RICARDO L. CASTRO

with essays by EDWARD DIMENDBERG, LAURENT STALDER AND GEORGES TEYSSOT

Arthur Erickson Critical Works

DOUGLAS & McINTYRE *Vancouver/Toronto*

VANCOUVER ART GALLERY

UNIVERSITY OF WASHINGTON PRESS *Seattle*

Douglas & McIntyre Ltd.
2323 Quebec Street, Suite 201
Vancouver, British Columbia
Canada V5T 4S7
www.douglas-mcintyre.com

Vancouver Art Gallery
750 Hornby Street
Vancouver, British Columbia
Canada V6Z 2H7
www.vanartgallery.bc.ca

Published simultaneously in the United States by
University of Washington Press
P.O. Box 50096
Seattle, WA 98145–5096 U.S.A.
www.washington.edu/uwpress

Project direction by Grant Arnold
Editing by Saeko Usukawa and Lucy Kenward
Jacket and text design by Peter Cocking
Jacket photographs by Ricardo L. Castro
Printed and bound in Canada by Friesens
Printed on acid-free paper

Douglas & McIntyre gratefully acknowledges the financial support of
the Canada Council for the Arts, the British Columbia Arts Council
and the Government of Canada through the Book Publishing Industry
Development Program (BPIDP) for our publishing activities.

Library and Archives Canada Cataloguing in Publication
Olsberg, Nicholas
Arthur Erickson : critical works / Nicholas Olsberg and Ricardo L.
Castro ; with essays by Edward Dimendberg, Laurent Stalder and
Georges Teyssot.

Co-published by Vancouver Art Gallery.
Includes bibliographical references and index.
ISBN-10: 1-55365-154-5 · ISBN-13: 978-1-55365-154-3

1. Erickson, Arthur, 1924–. I. Castro, Ricardo L.
II. Vancouver Art Gallery III. Title.
NA749.E74O48 2006   720'.92   C2005-904436-5

Library of Congress Cataloging-in-Publication Data
Olsberg, R. Nicholas.
Arthur Erickson : critical works / Nicholas Olsberg and
Ricardo L. Castro ; with essays by Edward Dimendberg,
Laurent Stalder and Georges Teyssot.
p. cm.
Includes bibliographical references and index.
ISBN 0-295-98620-4 (hardback : alk. paper)
1. Erickson, Arthur, 1924– —Criticism and interpretation.
I. Erickson, Arthur, 1924– II. Castro, Ricardo L. III. Title.
NA749.E74O47 2006
720.92—dc22
2006001350

The Vancouver Art Gallery gratefully acknowledges the support
of the City of Vancouver, the Province of British Columbia
through the BC Arts Council and Gaming Revenues, the
Government of Canada through the Canada Council for the
Arts, the Department of Canadian Heritage Museums Assistance
Program and Cultural Spaces Canada.

Financial assistance from the Canada Council for the Arts Pilot
Program in Architecture has supported the Arthur Erickson
exhibition and related public programs. The Graham Foundation
for Advanced Studies in the Fine Arts and L'institut de recherche
en histoire de l'architecture supported initial research for the
exhibition and this publication.

Contents

Foreword

ARTHUR ERICKSON has been widely acclaimed as the pre-eminent Canadian architect of the latter half of the twentieth century. Characterized by attention to physical context and truthfulness to materials, his work embodies an extraordinary range of cultural references while avoiding any sense of imitation or mimicry. Although Erickson's profile is global, he has maintained a close association with his home city of Vancouver throughout his career.

The relationship between the Vancouver Art Gallery and Arthur Erickson extends back to 1941, when a painting by the sixteen-year-old Erickson was selected for the Gallery's *10th Annual BC Artists Exhibition*. The Gallery subsequently mounted solo exhibitions of Erickson's architectural work in 1965 and 1985. Further, Erickson designed the transformation of the Gallery's current quarters from Provincial Courthouse to art museum in 1983 as part of the acclaimed Three Block Project. Given this long association, it is particularly gratifying for the Gallery to co-publish *Arthur Erickson: Critical Works* with Douglas & McIntyre and to present the accompanying exhibition that surveys his major accomplishments.

The Vancouver Art Gallery is deeply indebted to Nicholas Olsberg, former Director of the Canadian Centre for Architecture in Montreal, who assembled a distinguished group of writers and contributed several texts of his own to this publication, while ably fulfilling the role of guest curator for the exhibition. The Gallery extends its appreciation to Ricardo L. Castro of the School of Architecture at McGill University who produced the portfolios of compelling photographs that are such a crucial component of this project and also designed the exhibition installation. Ricardo and David Theodore, also of the School of Architecture at McGill University, wrote the evocative descriptions that complement the portfolios. We are very grateful to Edward Dimendberg of the University of California at Irvine, Laurent Stalder of the Swiss Federal Institute of Technology in Zurich and Georges Teyssot of Laval University, Quebec, for their insightful contributions to the literature on Erickson. David Theodore has illuminated important aspects of Erickson's work in his catalogue entries. The Gallery acknowledges the efforts of Saeko Usukawa and Lucy Kenward of Douglas and McIntyre, who edited the manuscripts; Peter Cocking, who produced the excellent design for this book, and Grant Arnold, Audain Curator of British Columbia Art at the Gallery, who has overseen the publication and exhibition. We are very grateful for the co-operation of the Canadian Centre for Architecture and the Canadian Architectural Archives, University of Calgary, in providing photographs for this publication and lending many of the objects that make up the exhibition.

Finally, we extend our profound appreciation to Arthur Erickson for his support, vision, enthusiasm, patience and, most importantly, the inspiration engendered through his architecture.

KATHLEEN S. BARTELS
Director, Vancouver Art Gallery

Introduction

OR MORE than forty years, Arthur Erickson has explored how architecture can "charge space with an inner presence and meaning,"[2] make "mundane materials…into something more evocative and powerful than the sum of their parts"[3] and dissolve boundaries between buildings, the design of cities and landscape architecture. He has read the landscape—built and natural—as a geography of time and space, with an underlying dynamic and an outlying structure, in which every major public work is a "miniature city"[4] and a laboratory for urban design. Urban works themselves are an exercise in anticipation, dealing with issues of growth "before they deal with us."[5] Above all, every project is bound to its "natural or man-made site" as part of "a panorama that may extend all the way to the horizon."[6]

That horizon broadens as we note Erickson's attention to the pattern and sensation of movement in a building. To him, this attention to the way we experience its anatomy, its vistas and its spatial passages, rather than its surface and structure, opens up "the spiritual dimension of architecture."[7] At the same time, his major works reassert architecture as a cultural practice concerned with invoking common associations, with making buildings—whether a museum, an embassy, a farmstead or a court of law—that open their purpose to view and with setting up more fluid crossroads for social interaction and the exchange of knowledge.

Erickson sees these factors as fundamental to the process of constructing a civil community. To achieve this, he has persistently viewed his brief on a project as something that "goes beyond the definition of requirements to the redefinition of purpose in the context of the society and the culture of that particular time and place" so that a building "injects into its culture a fresh response to its traditions."[8]

Erickson burst on the international scene in 1964 and '65, at the age of forty, with the widespread publication of photographs of his houses for David Graham and Gordon Smith and of his designs for the new Simon Fraser University. A rapid succession of public projects continued to gain him international recognition—the keynote pavilion at Expo 67, the University of Lethbridge in 1968 and, in 1970, both the prize-winning Canadian pavilion in Osaka and the MacMillan Bloedel office building in Vancouver. After 1972, a second burst of important projects appeared—the Helmut Eppich house (1974), the Museum of Anthropology (1976) and Robson Square (1978), all in Vancouver—keeping him securely in the currents of international discussion and debate. In 1980, Erickson won the contract for the massive Los Angeles downtown redevelopment project known as California Plaza and expanded his firm, which had established offices in Toronto in 1969 and in Saudi Arabia in 1975, into the United States.

"I am a Canadian, open to the broad world, and my work draws on universal sources to make a cultural mesh. But cultures must find their contexts, and those contexts must be recognized in the elusive as well as the apparent."[1]

ARTHUR ERICKSON

This expansion largely failed. Erickson struggled to accommodate the standardized components on which clients now insisted and, as a genuine scholar of the classical tradition, to adapt to the "transgression of history" that he saw in postmodernism.[9] His method, linked to reflection and dialogue, was ill-suited to economies of scale, collaboration, compromise and haste, and his insistence on the uniquely right solution was "immensely stimulating, but nothing could have been contrived to be less efficient."[10] It precluded the repeatable solutions that allowed large offices to address a huge project list. Alienated by the postmodernists and suspicious of new theoretical models, which he found too remote from the idea of visual instinct in which he trusted for design, Erickson became isolated from the intelligent discourse in which he belonged and "out of step with his times."[11] Starting in 1989, each of his offices slowly fell into bankruptcy and his practice was eventually curtailed by the courts. It took a full decade to revive.

In 1999, looking back over his career, Erickson identified his work as having three phases. First was the formative practice that ended in 1963, in which each work marked an experimental step towards mastering site, materials, space and context. Second came the sequence of work in partnership with Geoffrey Massey, starting with Simon Fraser University (1963–65), in which Erickson gradually matured a language closely linked to his love of concrete and achieved force and presence through a sort of absolute legibility and Doric simplicity. These are best exemplified in the office tower for MacMillan Bloedel (1965–70) and the great bridge structure at the University of Lethbridge (1968–70), where elaborate subtleties of plan, spatial progression and movement are subsumed into monolithic forms. After a short hiatus, during which work dwindled and the partnership dissolved, a third phase began in 1972 with the arrival of commissions in Vancouver for the Helmut Eppich house, the Museum of Anthropol-

ogy and the vast Three Block Project for a civic and cultural centre at Robson Square. With these projects, Erickson's work allowed more of its inherent layering and complexity to emerge. By the time of the design for Napp Laboratories and the Bagley Wright house, both of which began in 1979, an even greater range of expression and more specific cultural and symbolic references were woven into the schemes. Counterpoint and complexity became more evident; there is a range of finish, colour and texture; and the argument unfolds gradually rather than through an emphasis on the force of the whole, by capturing a changing theatre of light, space, movement and matter. The contributions of the landscape architect Cornelia Hahn Oberlander and of the interior designer Francisco Kripacz, who began their association with Erickson in the early 1970s, were essential to developing this more suggestive and varied palette. This period ended with the elaborate collages of Erickson's work in the Middle East, and at the Puget Sound house and Canadian Chancery, whose designs began in 1983.

With the revival of his practice at the turn of the new century, Erickson entered a fourth phase in which he recognizes a return to the uniform character of his work with Massey in the 1960s. But his recent work eschews the single-minded logic of those early monumental forms in favour of an apparently casual assembly of masses, in which an underlying symmetry, whose logic may stretch to the horizon, is scrupulously disguised. This simplified collage becomes fundamental to two late urban projects: the Tacoma Museum of Glass and the mixed-use Waterfall Building in Vancouver, both completed in 2002. These are "concrete landscapes in which the vocabulary has become simpler and simpler and simpler."[12]

Images of Erickson's great works of the 1960s and '70s remain firmly in architects' memories, and there is growing fascination with his approach to planning at a large scale. But it is now becoming apparent that Erickson also holds a crucial place among those architects—Le Corbusier and Louis Kahn are the prime examples—who were formed as modernists and were faithful to its fundamental premises of clarity of structure and simplicity of surface, but who moved away from its emotional neutrality to invest its truth to materials, geometries and structure with feeling and "presence." He himself speaks of "presence" in three ways. From the start, he noted that in the great buildings he saw on his travels the space "communicates a spiritual dimension—the presence of an inner life."[13] More gradually, he came to recognize in them, too, the presence of energy within repose, "a contained vitality like the stillness of the athlete or the dancer poised."[14] Finally, as he recognized how much his own work reflected his experiences and observations, Erickson identified a third presence in the fund of memory and association that gives voice to new forms—the "continuum" that sounds echoes of other histories and cultures into a building and connects it to the universal.[15]

Erickson's major works were designed to settle into contexts that had not quite emerged: a maturing landscape, the developing backdrop of a city centre or a growing campus. At the same time, concrete, the material behind the poetry of his essential work, needs to age before it can communicate that resonance with cultural memory that he intends us to sense within the forms and spaces he has moulded from it. And, in order to fully comprehend an architecture that is centrally concerned with opening spaces, grades and vistas to the moving figure or to a gathering crowd, his buildings need time to work out habits and patterns of use; to host conversations, celebrations and ceremonies, and to allow the landscapes that are central to their argument to mellow and mature.

This book, therefore, sets out to revisit in words and images twelve of Erickson's built works—ten now well matured—from which his critical arguments and his concrete poetry are most provocatively, variously and profoundly evident. All of them reflect the intimate spirit that characterizes the work of his Vancouver office: a reliance on the instinct for discovery and the elusive motion of "the unconscious ocean we carry within us"[16] rather than on an excess of analysis, system or reason. Erickson speaks of this method as a search for "motivation, the uncovering of a motif that is inherent in the context and will organize the composition"[17] and that comes as a "cathartic revelation," not from testing or inventing solutions but from relying on memory, feeling and "cultural confidence" to find a form that is "waiting to be discovered and transformed."[18] Only after does a logic and meaning become clear.

This approach is grounded in respect for the primacy of context in determining the nature of a work. Each is a wholly independent exercise that responds to its particular circumstance. But the twelve critical works here, even the Puget Sound house (where concrete underlies an exercise in archetypal wood and metal forms), all use structural concrete as their governing medium. Erickson says he has found in concrete his "muse": a substance from which to carve forms that open up recognition of the patterns and sources of our culture, heighten perceptions of earthly and celestial phenomena, and establish a different rhythm to the movements and meetings both between us, and between ourselves and our environs.

Thus siting, aesthetics and function are each given a cultural task which it would be meaningless to attempt to design without a foundation of knowledge. As the architect Giuseppe Mazzariol noted in 1968, Erickson is "as cultivated as any humanist of the Italian Cinquecento."[19] Calling him the "Hellenist of our times,"[20] Mazzariol drew attention to the breadth of Erickson's observations and to how it enables him to see continuity between cultures and times distant from his own, and resonance between generic patterns of civil community and the specific demands of current sites and programs. To this knowledge, Erickson adds an equal readiness to accept the unknown. He talks of civilization being a balance between "mysticism and materialism," of the need to "probe the unknowable,"[21] of "seeing through the brain rather than with the eyes"[22] and of "a floating, unselective frame of mind."[23] This is not a romantic belief in the supremacy of individual imagination but a conviction that culture and context should determine how a built form is shaped, and that the architect's task is to recognize that contextual prompting and make it legible: "Creation is not an invention but a discovery of what is."[24] "Context," Erickson says, "pervades the design so irrevocably that the building form is meaningless without it."[25]

ERICKSON WAS BORN in Vancouver, in 1924, into a cultivated, sociable and independent-minded family with a taste for the arts, who had moved from the tight Presbyterian society of Toronto at the end of the First World War in a conscious decision to seek a more democratic and relaxed society where "people took tolerance for granted, were optimistic about the future, and were not terribly bound by the past."[26] To provide a stimulating social and visual world that his father, who had lost both legs at Amiens, could readily negotiate, Erickson's childhood home was filled with landscape paintings, open to views and arranged to ease movement and to facilitate congregation. These factors—an intellectual self-confidence, nonconformity and sociability; a respect for culture, ceremony and the play of ideas; a readiness to look forward, and a fascination with mobility and vista—come into play throughout Erickson's work, marking his approach to constructing patterns of domestic and public life and to setting them in dialogue with their circumstances.

He spent much of his childhood drawing and painting from nature, and at fifteen he drew the attention of the Group of Seven painter Lawren Harris, who introduced him to a broad circle of progressive thinkers in the arts. Among them, Bert and Jessie Binning, with their wide knowledge of new music, European abstraction, primitivism and the arts of Japan, were signal leaders. Harris also awakened Erickson to a transcendental view of art and of the universe derived from a theosophical and Jungian base with which Erickson, though never attracted to its arcanities, remained in deep sympathy, and which quietly infuses the whole tenor of his inquiry into the purposes and processes of designing buildings. These different strains of avant-garde thinking in the arts—the scientific, Einsteinian dissolution of space and time that was so instrumental in forming cubist painting and the new rational and functional movements in architecture; the universalist, quasi-mystical sources of abstraction that generated the work of such artists as Mondrian and Kandinsky, and the inquiry into "primitive" art that appealed to both—were fundamental, and fundamentally reconcilable, in Erickson's view of the phenomena of nature and the universe. He talks of Einstein and cubism teaching him to "take things apart to reveal

4

Simplicity. Erickson describes his work in the 1960s as a progress towards reduction, and his latest work as "concrete landscapes, in which my vocabulary becomes simpler and simpler and simpler." Entrance to the Museum of Anthropology, Vancouver.

GOOD WISHES ARTHUR ERICKSON MEILLEURS VOEUX

them,"[27] of the role of "primitive art" in showing the internal structure of natural forms and of both in helping him to replace the Renaissance convention of perspective in favour of an "x-ray vision." At the same time, Erickson learned from Kandinsky and Harris, and would soon reinforce through his reading of Frank Lloyd Wright and his experience of the culture of Japan, another level of discernment that could grasp an invisible dimension in things, including things made by the human hand, that expressed their unique properties and might address a world beyond them.

It was in this spirit that the eighteen-year-old Erickson asked the modernist architect Richard Neutra, who visited Vancouver in 1942, how to become an architect "as an artist,"[28] and on being told to go to the Massachusetts Institute of Technology and study engineering, abandoned that pursuit and went to the University of British Columbia to take a general degree in the arts. There, he grounded himself quite deeply in two fields that would inform his work: political economy, and Asian languages and linguistics. He had begun further study of Japanese when military service took him to India and Malaya for two years. Upon his return, a publication about Wright's Taliesin West came as a revelation, reawakening his interest in architecture, and he enrolled at McGill University in Montreal. History was taught through Siegfried Giedion's book *Space, Time, and Architecture*; classes went to Boston to visit the Walter Gropius and Marcel Breuer studios, and the teachers introduced students to the work and writings of Le Corbusier, to which Erickson responded with enormous enthusiasm. But he describes the studio methods at McGill as constricting, always insisting on "starting from the 'good'" when Erickson wanted to muddy the waters by "seeing what happened, 'good' or 'bad,'" and he learned far more about the process of design from the art and graphics teacher, Gordon Webber, who "never saw what others saw," who encouraged the "idiosyncratic eye" and who grounded teaching in Laszlo Moholy-Nagy's method of "creative play."[29]

At the end of his degree, Erickson considered an apprenticeship with Wright, but was awarded a travelling scholarship to Europe from McGill. He left Canada in the summer of 1950 and, for more than two years, followed a progress—ancient to modern and south to north—through architectural history, visiting Egypt, Syria, Greece, Italy, Spain and France, concluding with the modern extravaganza of the 1951 Festival of Britain. He met such luminaries as architects Ernesto Rogers and Denys Lasdun, and learned from others: Giuseppe Terragni's use of concrete as a frame, and the contrapuntal play between Terragni's Casa del Fascio and the old city of Como are prime examples. But it was the archaic and vernacular and elements of the archaic as they began to appear within the modern, like Le Corbusier at Ronchamp, that had the profoundest effect. Erickson was less interested in the individual faces of buildings than in their "unfoldings" of volume and void or of ensemble and passage, like the juxtapositions on an ancient acropolis or on the terraces of vines and lemon trees that stepped down the hill below an Italian villa. And later, in all his urban work, he would draw upon the memory of the medieval townscape, the streets of the Mediterranean village or the undulating pedestrianism of Venice, and on their central lesson: that a building lives only in relation to its neighbours.[30]

In Erickson's early work, identifiable shapes, plans and forms occasionally appear as conscious reminiscences, like the Andalusian columns of his Dal Grauer cabana or the suggestions of pierced screens at the Filberg house. More frequently, the recollection of an ancient source inspires the dominant element that generates the larger scheme in all his work after 1963. Such is the indirect role of the palaestra of Pergamon in the composition of the Simon Fraser gymnasium or of the circular Romanesque churches of France in the form of its lantern. Columns, pediments, capitals, arches and towers derived from these ancient sources appear again briefly in his work of the 1980s, first as a nod to the requirements of projects in the Middle East and then to correct the postmodernists by demonstrating how to translate histori-

cist elements at truer scale and purpose.[31] Indeed, in works like the Puget Sound house, Erickson confesses a debt to the postmodern he despised by taking it as permission "to render more literally the classical canons I have loved since 1950."[32]

But what he took most from his travels and observations were ineffable, largely buried "memories of space" on which his instinct would draw as he sought to reach "a sense of doing what is right and necessary, of gaining an unconscious architecture."[33] They might catch him by surprise only long after completion, and as a consonance of feeling rather than form. It was only after looking at the completed front of the Museum of Anthropology as it turns towards the water—a gaze he thought he had drawn from the totem pole—that he realized he had actually "captured the force of ancient Egypt—the face of the gods staring like a sphinx, impassively into the wilderness."[34]

By the time Erickson returned to Vancouver to start his career, he was nearly thirty, and Vancouver was a different city. There had been a massive influx of Europeans, architects and engineers among them; the city's leading commercial design firms had adopted the language of modernism; new suburbs and low-cost housing were springing up to accommodate veterans' families; a school of architecture was forming at the University of British Columbia; there was a rage for rethinking the city plan, its centre and its arteries; and a flood of young designers, who had trained in the modern schools and had heard that architectural adventures might be afoot, were arriving to take advantage of its building boom. Erickson worked with a number of the leading offices, but from

facing page: Presence. Believing that buildings at their best are "charged with contained vitality," Erickson sketched the Museum of Anthropology in 1972–74 to express this sense of its electricity. He was surprised to discover that his efforts to make a building consonant with the totemic power of Northwest Coast Native art "had, in fact, captured the force of ancient Egypt." The sketch was subsequently used on a greeting card.

1953 onward, he maintained a steady practice of his own, in loose association with Geoffrey Massey, who had arrived, at the same time, from the Harvard School of Design. Winning a national prize with their first work, a house for the artist Gordon Smith, Erickson was able to maintain a steady flow of domestic and small-scale commercial work for the next ten years.

In 1956, he went to the University of Oregon to teach for a year and, in 1957, began an association with the University of British Columbia. This contact with students allowed him to develop the cadre of a small-scale architectural services practice the following year, and the first work of this office, the house in the landscape of Vancouver Island for Robert Filberg, drew considerable attention. The pedagogic system at Oregon, which trusted to aesthetic instinct and an uncritical dialogue, struck a chord with the young architect, who had found himself at odds with the systematic approach at McGill, and it became Erickson's own method, not only in his teaching but also in working with his associates. He opposed the regionalist movement that had grown up between San Francisco and Vancouver, realizing that his own quest for universal forms in specific contexts called not for settling quietly into the landscape with subtle craftsmanship but for engaging it in a more assertive conversation. Much of the work of the next five years was concerned with finding a voice, and a language of site and matter, that escaped both the "banality and neutrality"[35] that modernist standardization risked and the potential sentimentality of the regionalists.

Each of the works in what Erickson describes as this "evolutionary" decade built on the one before, testing the nature of materials and the formal and structural qualities that suited them, and exploring new possibilities in siting and plan. The 1956 Dal Grauer cabana uses translucent fibreglass to test traditional forms against new scales and contexts. The 1958 Filberg house mixes many materials and elements in a new discussion of light, weightlessness, flow and vista. Both are self-consciously neo-Romantic. The 1960 housing complex at Point Grey retreats from transparency and lightness towards more solidity and shows a rethinking of the boundaries between common space and private. Weight, shelter and shadow are advanced with the Dyde, Danto and Fuldauer houses of 1960–63, which settle onto the ground with decisive topographies of their own. Detail becomes less important; shape starts to show plan; blank walls manage enclosure and roof openings, light. There is increasing thrust and movement.

Erickson's long trip to Japan in 1961 "radicalized" him, producing a "clarification" of his work, in which "detail disappeared" and everything was made servant to "purity of form."[36] In Japan, he saw for the first time the textured and opaque poetics inherent in concrete. Concrete had been almost the only material there with which to rebuild a war-devastated urban landscape, and the Japanese had learned to appreciate the richness of its surface and the strength of its expression of form. It was treated as he had never seen it before, "with frankness."[37] With this medium, he could see himself doing what he had so admired in Greece, Egypt and Syria: carving out his buildings from the matter of which they were made, and then carving them with that matter into the sites they held, for concrete held the ground plane as richly as it made the wall. Indeed, Erickson regards his Middle Eastern designs—more than twenty public projects that began in

1975, of which only unsupervised variants were ever built—as "the apotheosis of concrete."[38] In a sunlit landscape against a yellow ground and among neighbours of rammed and battered earth, it seems to come home. But concrete seems equally sympathetic to the white skies and greyer tones of the Pacific Northwest, warming them where it cools the heat of the Arabian peninsula. Erickson constantly tested forms in other materials, but they nearly all adapt into concrete or into a relationship with it. The simple assembly of uniform heavy wood beams at the Tokyo 65 international trade fair, at Expo 67 and in the Fire Island house of 1977 all translate to in situ concrete in projects such as the pyramidal terrace of the Evergreen building. The moulding of steel and glass at the Hugo Eppich house of 1979 tests a solution for the use of concrete at the Napp Laboratories two years later, and is converted into the play between steel, glass and concrete in the vaulting forms of the San Diego Convention Center of 1981. Reflective glass at Osaka 70 and in the proposals for Christ Church Cathedral of 1973 start to develop the shapes and tones of the reflective pavilions that give life to the concrete plinths and plazas of Roy Thomson Hall, Tacoma Museum of Glass and the Waterfall Building.

Erickson has ultimately made more of concrete, as Mies van der Rohe made more of steel and glass, by using it in a way that speaks to nothing else, coffering and coving it, eliminating even the trace of formwork to render its simplicity, letting it make the structure be seen plain, and shaping it equally into pathway or frame, wall or plaza, to make a common concrete landscape. These confidently democratic landscapes seem to match a time in which Canada itself was asserting the sort of geographical inclusiveness and social transparency that Erickson's work advances—his most adventurous public work was closely associated with the international liberalism of Lester Pearson and Pierre Trudeau or the socialist policies of the New Democrats of western Canada. Perhaps Erickson's own "cultural confidence"[39] could best flourish in a Canada where the idea that "civilization" could be at once embraced and reformed might be adopted without cynicism, where diverse traditions were treated with studied respect, and where the idea could be advanced without skepticism that wild and made landscapes, the mystic and the real, the known and unknowable, could all still be reconciled. His works are the concretization of that generous and optimistic "culture in context."

NOTES

1. Arthur Erickson, in discussion with the author, 1999–2004.

2. Ibid.

3. Arthur Erickson, *The Architecture of Arthur Erickson* (Vancouver/Toronto: Douglas & McIntyre, 1988), 12.

4. Edith Iglauer, "Profiles: Seven Stones," *New Yorker,* June 4, 1979, 42–86.

5. Arthur Erickson, interview with Trevor Boddy, "Erickson's Vancouver: Cityscape I," *Vancouver Sun,* June 12, 2004.

6. Peter Blake in Erickson, *The Architecture of Arthur Erickson,* 10–11.

7. Erickson, discussion with author. See also Michael McMordie in *Contemporary Architects,* Muriel Emanuel, ed. (New York: St. Martin's Press, 1992), 289–90.

8. *Contemporary Architects,* 289.

9. Erickson, discussion with author.

10. Bing Thom (Vancouver-based architect), in discussion with the author, 2001.

11. Erickson, discussion with author.

12. Ibid.

13. Ibid.

14. Ibid.

15. Giuseppe Mazzariol, "Il linguaggio di Erickson," *Lotus* 5 (1968), 168–87. (trans. Nicholas Olsberg)

16. Arthur Erickson, *Thoughts on Architecture: A Personal View,* unpublished manuscript at the Canadian Centre for Architecture, Montreal, 1999.

17. Erickson, discussion with author.

18. Erickson, discussion with author. See also Erickson, *Thoughts on Architecture: A Personal View.*

19. Mazzariol, 161.

20 Ibid.

21. Erickson, *Thoughts on Architecture: A Personal View.*

22. Erickson, discussion with author.

23. Iglauer, 44.

24. Arthur Erickson, *Habitation: Space, Dilemma, and Design,* pamphlet published by Canadian Housing Design Council, Ottawa, 1966, with an appendix, 1967.

25. *Contemporary Architects,* 289.

26. Erickson, *The Architecture of Arthur Erickson,* 17.

27. Erickson, discussion with author.

28. Ibid.

29. Erickson, *Habitation: Space, Dilemma, and Design.*

30. Erickson, discussion with author. See also Arthur Erickson, unpublished draft of memoirs. Used by permission of the author.

31. Erickson, discussion with author.

32. Ibid.

33. Erickson, unpublished memoirs and Erickson, discussion with author.

34. Erickson, discussion with author.

35. Ibid.

36. Ibid.

37. Arthur Erickson, "The Weight of Heaven," *Canadian Architect* 9 (1964), 48–53.

38. Erickson, discussion with author.

39. Ibid.

Infinity

"The Shape of God and the Worth of Man"

Arthur Erickson has always insisted that the essence of architecture is in the dialogue wrought by bringing a building and its setting into conversation, and he has suggested that, at its most successful, this discussion between the small finite building and the large indefinite circumstance of its situation can establish a perception of the "infinities" to which they both belong. This sense that a work of architecture acquires a special charge by implying the indeterminate or by unfolding the boundless is most evident in Erickson's small-scale work within the landscape, and it clearly draws from his own dialogue with the settings in which he was raised, formed and worked.

The landscape of wide inlets, forested islands and high mainland peaks that are the setting for the city of Vancouver is black and off-white, silver and shades of grey; it is not contoured but is a set of planes, vertical and horizontal, like a stage floor broken by platforms, with a lightly painted backdrop of imprecise white glaciers and snowcaps. The islands and the mountains may seem to close it in, but it is a world without clear boundaries or edges, extending who can say how far. There is little change between the tones of the sky and the water, except that one is usually dense and the other reflective, so that the horizon between them is just a soft line between two textures. In this environment, the smaller the domestic enclosure, the larger the unending sense of the ele-

ments beyond it: the grey scrim of the sky, the silver mirror of the waters and the nearly lightless forest. Not just the sun, but light itself, Erickson said, "is remote and hidden above the clouds."[2]

There are human references, too, in Erickson's readiness to capture a gaze upon this "hidden remote." There are reflections of the work of his boyhood mentor, the artist Lawren Harris, who, when Erickson knew him, was moving from paintings that were reading the infinite obliquely, within the primal earthly landscape of the northwest, to those that were imagining it in the generative terms of a fundamental cosmic geometry. Although Erickson awoke to the full intelligence of Northwest Coast Native art, and especially the totem pole, only later, his study of Asian linguistics and his familiarity with the artist Emily Carr and the school of West Coast painting had readied him to recognize in that Native art a symbolic language that addresses aspects of the eternal and unknowable—the infinity of time in its stylization of natural forms, and the space beyond in the way the human-built was sited and disposed in the landscape. Erickson's conviction that architecture, too, is a symbolic language grew from such sources, and it is for how that symbolic system might represent similar intangibles—space, time, infinity, the "weight of heaven"[3]—that he values it and works towards its mastery.

From his first visit to Japan in 1961, he found a second home of covered skies, of rain, mists and "soft light on the

"The act of siting betrays to us the tenor of human aspiration, the shape of God and the worth of man."[1]

ARTHUR ERICKSON

forest floor."[4] It was, he noted, a culture in which the vast chords of time, mood and space could speak through things made or arranged by an artist in however small and domestic a form: William Blake's "world in a grain of sand." Acknowledging, however, that Japan's modes of thought and culture were very different, and that architecture could "invest mute forms with meaning only by being true to its own circumstance and place,"[5] Erickson began to seek a vocabulary of siting, form and material through which he might capture a sense of the infinite that was true to his own. He built almost unconsciously upon three broad concepts he had recognized in Japan: that a built structure, especially if it drew no attention to its own crafting, might not only complement the natural features of its surroundings but actively unfold their qualities; that darkness, recession and shadow could be made to imply infinite depth; and that a flat plane, or the ground itself, could be cut into, textured or layered to suggest its buried strata—temporal, vegetal and mineral.

The complex roots and strategies of Erickson's inquiry into how to reach the infinite can be seen as he turned his own garden into something like a three-dimensional Japanese print or screen—painting, within the compass of the eye and the confines of a suburban lot, a vast natural world. Only once he had started to shift its contours did Erickson begin to see, so he said later, that the character of his garden was "a forest clearing," where the eye needed to journey through light to gain a sense of "greater space."[6] Depth and time expand as we follow light receding over dappled water, unconsciously pause for the voyage we imagine it takes to cross, then reach the forest shadows of a profoundly black distance. Nothing illustrates more clearly what Erickson meant when he said that "qualities of light… are the well-springs of feelings

which the Orient senses better than we. With light as the palette…we can bring soul and spirit back into architecture and perhaps find our own souls in the process."[7]

WITH THE SECOND HOUSE that Erickson designed for Gordon and Marion Smith, in 1964 in West Vancouver, he found himself ready to draw fully on the heightened awareness that Japan had given him. By "putting the house together with rough fir beams direct from the mill" and assembling it "in a rudimentary structural way like a log cabin"[8] or a Native house, he was adapting the ideas of "vacancy" inherent in the Japanese tea house, recognizing, as he said, that "in the Taoist sense it is only vacancy that can be filled."[9] One side of the house suggests the protective sense of a walled mass entered almost at grade, a cabin in a clearing. The other is transparent and seems weightless and suspended, like a Japanese garden pavilion. The reconciliation of open and closed—necessary in this towering wilderness and necessary to each other to gain their force—is thus achieved through passing from one to the other in a journey for which light is the essential context.

It is interesting to see how differently Erickson, working with architect Geoffrey Massey, treated another West Vancouver site in the house for David Graham, completed the year before. Where the Smith house wanders serenely around itself, the Graham house steps down its steep site towards the sea by means of a set of overlapping roofs that could themselves be shelves of water, like the terraced gardens of the Villa d'Este. The heavy overhanging beams set up a deliberate tension with the narrow columns on which they sit, just as the flat roof planes and broad jutting beams are set off against the mounded topography beneath them and the

Arthur Erickson and Geoffrey
Massey, Gordon Smith House,
West Vancouver (1964).

spiky filigree of the surrounding firs. The Craig house, built by Erickson/Massey at the same time, is set in the sparser landscape and sharper light of the Okanagan in the interior of British Columbia. Its concrete supports and walls play against wooden posts and beams to echo the random juxtapositions of dry earth, rock and timber; space is organized as a descending set of interlocking pavilions that follow the slope. Ten years later, the two approaches—discovering the boundless through vigour, contrast and collage (as in the Graham and Craig houses) as well as through repetition, perambulation and repose (as in the second Smith house)—came together in the house for Helmut Eppich and in the Museum of Anthropology.

Meanwhile, Erickson used his pavilions for the world's fairs in Tokyo (1965) and Montreal (1967) to test how far the ruthless assembly of regular lengths of the same rough-cut material might be worked into symbolic geometries to express the sublime. Both were conceived as "lumber piles" built "without any elegance at all"[10] to intensify their roles as a form of window on nature. Inside the Montreal pavilion, the dark pile served as a gigantic roof that covered a little oasis Erickson called a "miniature Eden."[11] It was a double expression of infinity in which the two scales of his domestic work—small building and large garden—were reversed.

For the Vancouver office of Erickson/Massey, finished in 1970, Erickson took the shell of a simple concrete-block warehouse, covered it with glass and dropped onto it a vast roof of wooden boards that sat, like a huge garden umbrella without a garden, on freestanding posts and angled struts of rough-sawn fir. In this extraordinary inversion of the Montreal pavilion, the rough wood structure drew in the light and

pushed it around itself like a corona, leaving all sense of recession, of the infinite, to be suggested either by disguise (hiding the source of light behind the wood roof) or by illusion (using greenery and the play of light to dissolve the solid opacity of the boundary walls).

A house in Ontario for Dick and Laurette Hilborn was initiated in 1970 by the Erickson/Massey office but completed by Erickson alone. The site was on a wooded slope falling sharply to a river, in a landscape of mixed deciduous woods and evergreens, undulating meadowlands, red earth and red-brick houses. Erickson oriented the house towards the drop but laid it close to the grade, setting its spaces out as a staggered sequence of shallow landings. They are each topped by flat wooden roofs that float in the landscape; they are enclosed by glass end walls that seem to carry the floors out into the grounds and by huge brick panels into which the roofs are set. The result feels not so much like a set of rooms as the interstices between a processional row of torii at a hilltop shrine, simply covered for shelter. This sense of having been constructed within an existing pattern of growth—human and natural—lends the house a temporal infinity in sympathy with a landscape of changing lights and seasons.

In freeing its built components from their functional roles as a system of enclosure in order to realize their sculptural and symbolic roles as expressions of pattern in the landscape, the Hilborn house shows Erickson's stated desire to "break apart traditional volumes" so that the planes and voids that constitute them could be "liberated."[12] Granted such independence, a simple repeated form, so long as it derived from an intuitive reading of its circumstances, could lend a building both "an inner presence" and the possibility of "intimating an infinite extension of itself."[13] This difficult idea, already inherent in Erickson's huge concrete works at the University of

Lethbridge in Alberta and the MacMillan Bloedel head office building in Vancouver, came to govern all his critical work in concrete in the years to come.

EARLY IN 1972, Helmut Eppich approached Erickson to design a house for a large steep lot in a gully on the upper slopes of West Vancouver. Erickson realized, as he began work, that concrete's relationship to earth, its opacity and its texture, were uniquely capable of helping him to generate shapes to "clarify" their setting. At Eppich (and later at the Bagley Wright house), it is as if the architect, having cut into the site to find its true character, moulded into concrete what he had removed from it, laid out that material above the ground into a monochromatic distillation of how to read the site that it came from, then gently reassembled the surroundings to reinforce the same inner logic. In both houses, the repeating geometries of the concrete forms heighten the force and independence of the buildings, as timber could not. Although they take their cues from a reading of the site, their dense hard lines serve not to echo the landscape but to concentrate and compact it, bringing the terrain into focus and crystallizing even its sense of boundlessness into hard-edged form.

The house steps down from the street to an entrance level in which the bedrooms are placed, then to a living plane of indoor and outdoor spaces, and finally to a platform that juts out over a reflective pond. Like the Hilborn house, and reminiscent of Frank Lloyd Wright's Fallingwater, the width and sequence of each terrace plane is irregular, governed by its relation to the topography and by Erickson's intent to "stretch the house out on varied planes, staggering them to suggest infinity at either end."[14] The essential vertical motif is simple: absolutely uniform repeated concrete frames, glazed or open, whose mathematical regularity, as they stride into the hills at

either side, suggests that they might go on forever. To the same end, Erickson made light sheer through skylights or dance through screens to dissolve the edges of the building, preventing a focus on the windowed walls and bringing light into the house as "a constant reminder of the movement of the sun."[15] The Eppich house plays upon the subtle tension between the random and the mathematical, the intuitive and the logical, the soft and the hard, rough wood and raw concrete.

As initial designs for the Eppich house were being completed, the first studies for the University of British Columbia Museum of Anthropology began, and the two projects, both finished in 1978, are parallel. Set atop cliffs at the outermost point of a peninsula, the museum works with the same symbolic ambitions and many of the same strategies. Erickson started from four premises. First was a belief that climate is "the major moderator of culture,"[16] an idea that inhabits all Erickson's theoretical writing. The sequence of objects was to follow a movement from southern cultural flamboyance to northern austerity. Second was the principle that water is essential as a boundary for totem poles, and that the mediation between sea and forest is the central function of a Northwest Coast Native village. Third was the idea that "light itself is a context."[17] Last was the idea, drawn from his experience of South Asian temples, that a museum of Native art must reconcile sacred space with public passage, allowing visitors both to observe what is there and to feel what is not.

Erickson, therefore, laid out a sequence of totem poles, moving from the southern to the northern cultures and letting the heights of the poles determine the lines both of the glass "canopy" that would light them and of the floor that would hold them. Just as the totem poles, like the "caryatids

facing page, photo: Vancouver office of Arthur Erickson Architects (1968). Photo by Dick Busher, Cosgrove Editions.

facing page, top sketch: Arthur Erickson, sketch of Graham House, West Vancouver (1963).

facing page, far right: Arthur Erickson, sketch of Hilborn House, Cambridge, Ontario (1974).

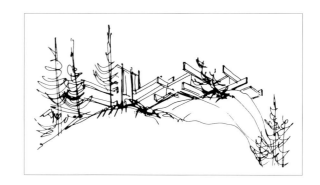

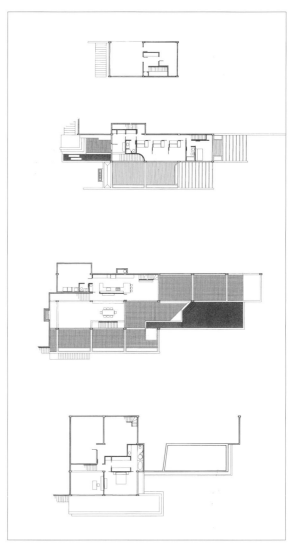

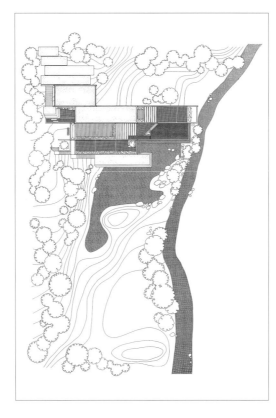

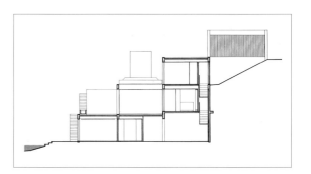

above: The 5500-square-foot Helmut Eppich house (Eppich I), completed in 1974, occupies a hillside site in West Vancouver, British Columbia. The terrace at the lower level of the house extends into the pond. Erickson published this photograph, taken immediately after construction, to show the "reach of the house into the landscape."

right: There is a difference in level of 40 feet between the access road and the lowest level, where Erickson diverted a stream to form a large artificial pond. He established the boundaries of the landscape before he designed the house, organizing the structure around the pond. Design team: Nick Milkovich.

far right, top: These plans show how the house steps down the hill from the access road in a series of indoor rooms, outdoor terraces and a swimming pool.

far right, bottom: The house is Erickson's first in concrete. This section reveals that he used it for retaining walls, and for beams and columns that recall his earlier use of timber.

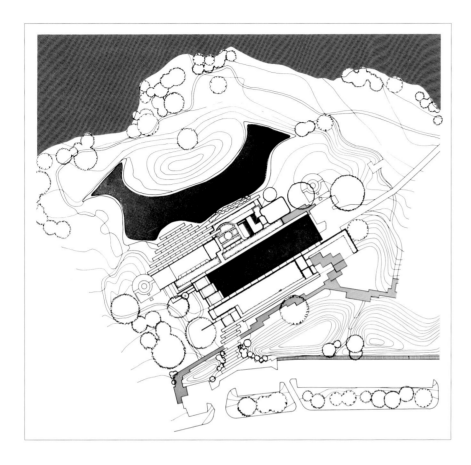

top: The Museum of Anthropology opened in 1976 at the University of British Columbia, Vancouver. The museum is a teaching facility for the university, containing academic classrooms, laboratory facilities and offices. Erickson based the organization of the site on a Haida waterfront village: outside the museum are two Haida houses and ten totem poles. The landscape design, by Cornelia Hahn Oberlander, features indigenous plants and grasses.

bottom: In this early model, Erickson proposed a pond to advance the idea of a First Nations precinct and to act as a reflecting pool for the dramatic north facade. The designers gradually diminished the pool's size to develop a landscape of shoreline, stony ground, grassy mounds and forest hinterland. Concerned about adverse effects on the ecology of the neighbouring historic Point Grey cliffs, however, university officials have left the pond area dry. Project team: Ron Bain, Alex Kee, Nick Milkovich, Barry Simpson, Freeman Chan.

on the Acropolis… stare out to the distant unknown," so the face of the museum itself looks away to the distant sea, to the sky, to the north, and "at nothing."[18] The rhythmic cascade of beams and posts turns and rises in a pattern that Erickson later recognized as Asian, akin to those used in Indian architecture and music, in the drumbeats of Japan and in the descending eaves of a pagoda. The concrete posts and beams, a "succession of frames—from low and wide to narrow and tall,"[19] recalling the frames of a Native house, and the repetition of the frame suggests a rhythm that might go on forever.

Later, with the Montiverdi Estates in West Vancouver in 1979, Erickson brought the idea of huge repeating frames into a domestic setting, developing a suburban variant on a Haida village. And that same year, in a house for Helmut Eppich's brother, Hugo, Erickson domesticated and adapted the glass roof of the great hall of the Museum of Anthropology into huge repeating arches of glass and bent steel that "leap outward into the land."[20] The house is a cascade of three open pavilions, as confident, tenuous and extroverted in greeting the landscape and as cheerful in its embrace of light

Arthur Erickson, section drawing of Hugo Eppich (Eppich II) House, West Vancouver (1979).

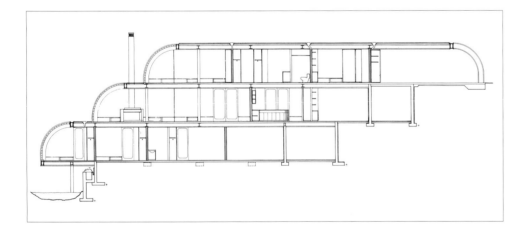

as the Helmut Eppich house, a cascade of three monumental caves, is contained, solid and quiet. Both experiments bear upon the forms and conversations with the land in the two houses that follow in Puget Sound, the first for Virginia and Bagley Wright.

Virginia Wright had begun collecting contemporary art with the purchase of a Mark Rothko work in 1951, and in 1977 she began talking to Erickson about a house in which to live with this collection. The site was north of Seattle, forested with tall cedars and firs, and set above an inlet of Puget Sound. Erickson's critical decisions were to cut a narrow swath through the forest from the water; to set the house on two shallow planes, backing up to and over a drop to the inlet, so that its base, focus and extensions would move into the landscape rather than towards the sea; to strip the trunks of the trees beside the swath to render them as architectonic forms; to cut the swath over, rather than into, the line of a shallow gradient on the site; to think of the principal space of the house—gallery, reception and living—as a swath itself, a wide axis cut through walls, lit from above and open at either end; to move these openings out onto surfaces—ponds, lawns, platforms—that would allow the house to "reach out to engage the surroundings."[21] Platforms and walls extending into the grounds, as well as the height and width of walls in the great interior hall, and the rhythms in which light and gaze would fall upon them, were all calibrated to specific works of art. As in the great hall of the Museum of Anthropology, the house's purpose was to set the logic and scale of the sculptures in conversation with that of the environment around them, to provide a "clearing" in which to illuminate art that was made to capture a reading of the infinite.

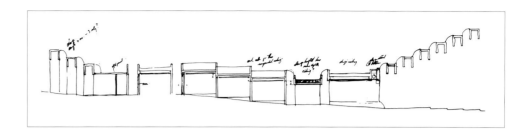

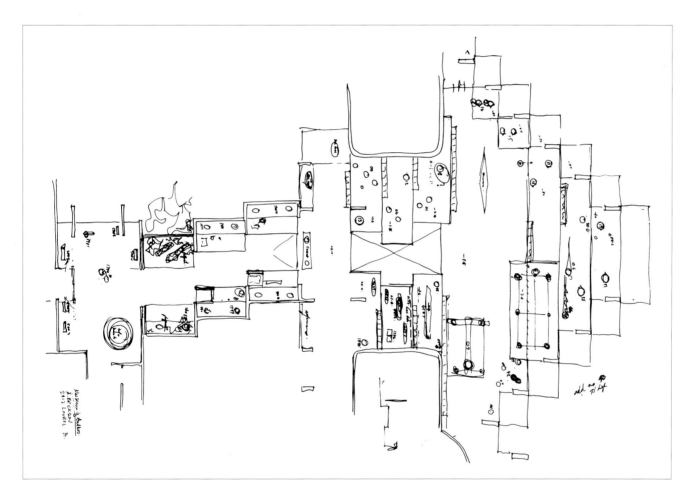

above: Erickson's felt-tip pen sketch of the north-south section of the Museum of Antropology shows a series of structural concrete post-and-beam gates framing the main circulation path. Visitors flow from the entry down to the great hall, where the beams of the frames, separated by curved acrylic skylights, sit as much as 49 feet above the ground and reach 180 feet in length. The north facade, a glass curtain wall, allows a panoramic view of the exterior.

left: The 66,000-square-foot museum houses an extensive collection of Northwest Coast First Nations art. Smaller objects are displayed in low-ceilinged galleries; the giant totem poles, 12 to 40 feet in height, face north towards the sea. The project incorporates three World War II concrete gun emplacements; one, on the interior, forms the base for Bill Reid's cedar sculpture *The Raven and the First Men.*

right: Completed in 1981, the
9000-square-foot Bagley Wright
residence north of Seattle,
Washington, occupies a wooded
9-acre site oriented east-west
towards Puget Sound. The house
sits in an artificial clearing
100 feet wide and 600 feet long.
Cornelia Hahn Oberlander's
landscape design included replacing the felled trees with plantings
of wildflowers. Design team:
Nick Milkovich, Inara Kundzins,
Allen Cheng, Bob Hoshide,
Sandra Fraser.

below: These sketch plans show
the conceptual organization of the
house. Three main zones run the
length of the house: guest quarters, a central public living and
dining area that extends to the
pool, and a private zone for the
master bedroom and staff.

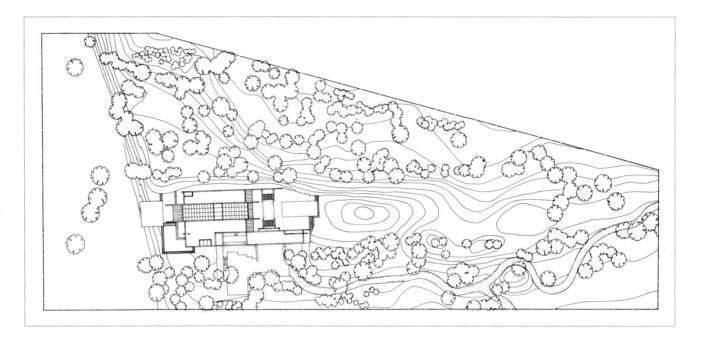

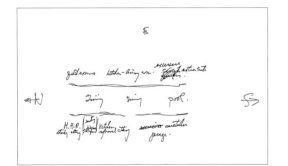
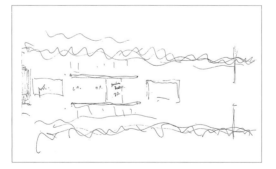
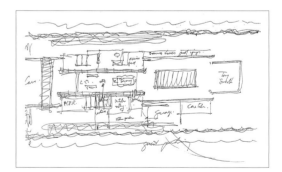

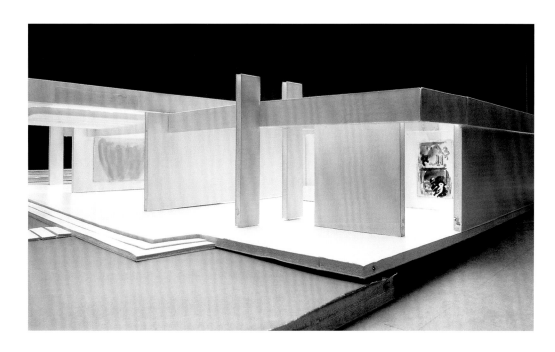

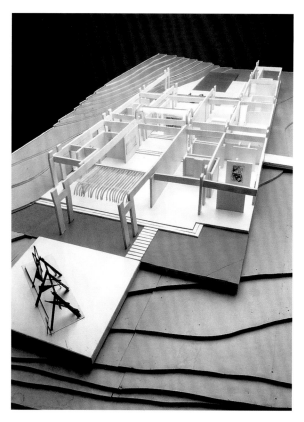

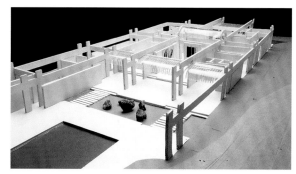

The models of the Bagley Wright house show two influences on the design: the desire to form an appropriate setting for the client's stunning collection of modern art, and the conceptual correspondence between the interior of the house and its setting in a clearing in the woods that is lit from above.

Erickson says the site itself "told us what and where the structure should be": an H plan. His task was to "abstract and edit" what the site prompted, "reducing the whole to as few elements—material, formal, structural—as possible... making the structure a point of reference and reflection on its own setting."[22] Nevertheless, the house embodies a set of perhaps instinctive references, not only synthesizing Erickson's own previous work but recalling the great swath that looks across water to the sunset at Louis Kahn's Salk Institute and the barrel skylights of his Kimbell Museum in Fort Worth. But the Bagley Wright house stands on its own, with a stunning simplicity in its approach to nature, as Erickson's own favourite work and the sum of his sense of the act of "clarification,... setting a structure into its surroundings... to gain the most poignant understanding of its larger circumstance."[23]

Just as work on the Bagley Wright house was being finished, another client commissioned a house, also on Puget Sound, in 1983. The site is a varied and rustic one of farmland and forest. In counterpoint to it, the house is a scattered assemblage of loosely vernacular forms marked by raw surfaces, sturdy geometries and casual relationships, both to each other and to their setting. Erickson moved only gradually towards the informal distribution of the house into distinct pavilions and towards the farmhouse language of wood and stone. Earlier, for the Wilson Bradley house in southern California in 1979, Erickson had adapted the H-plan of the Bagley Wright project within a single symmetrical precinct of concrete columns and walls set on a flat pad of stone paving. This he placed on a podium, ignoring the grade and allowing the house simply to sit like a platform on its brow, gaining a sense of extension by opening vistas to the groves around it.

The Bradley house was Erickson's Mediterranean reminiscence, and it was in the same spirit that he began the Puget Sound house, with Palladian villas, the Parthenon, masonry and concrete in mind. In the final version of the Puget Sound house, however, what was left of this classical language, after Erickson had stripped it down and dispersed its elements, conjured up something quite different: a child's toy farm or a village. Indeed, according to Cornelia Hahn Oberlander, the distribution of the elements into, around and under the landscape was consciously designed for an extended family in "constant motion and ready for surprise."[24]

Although the Puget Sound compound thus advanced Erickson's conversations with the landscape, it also moved him away from two decades of essentially abstract elements, realized through concrete poured in place, to a mixed palette of materials and into a short excursion into a more literal use of archaic forms, though one in which these mnemonic motifs took on a new and provocative life through shifts in scale and the use of uncharacteristic tones and textures, and, just as they are scattered informally into the landscape, through juxtapositions into a collage.

Erickson turned to another set of historical archetypes in a house for Vinod and Neeru Khosla in the Portola Valley of California. The house cascades in two wings of intimate space gently down from the crest of a hill, on which sits the living area, a single room with a grand and precipitate prospect away from the house. In a reminiscence of India and the Near East, columns are clustered to frame these wings and to support a glass pavilion that covers the space between them and shelters a terraced concrete watercourse. One face of the house suggests a North American ideal of infinity comprehended through the spectacle of drop and panorama. The other, as in the Moghul gardens and Sufic lyrics on which the

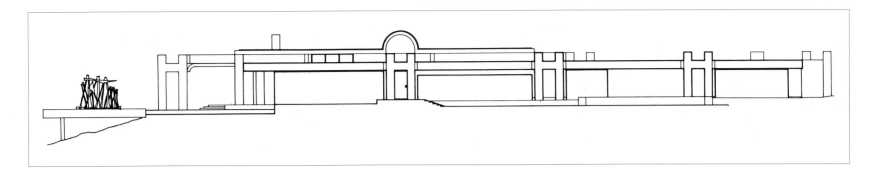

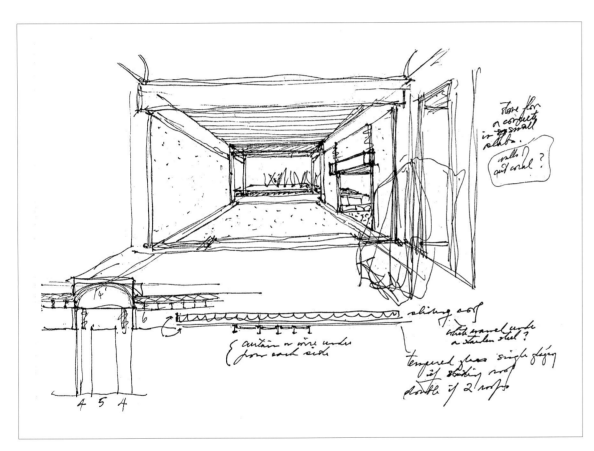

above: The section of the Bagley Wright house shows the regular proportioning of the interior spaces and the structure of the concrete H-shaped double columns. The priority given to the owners' collection of contemporary art is manifest here in the initial placement of the Anthony Caro sculpture *Riviera* outside the house, cantilevered just beyond the main living area. An innovative sand-blasted 2200-square-foot glass-block ceiling provides filtered natural light.

left: Erickson's sketch shows a view through the central living area out towards the Caro sculpture. Notes detail ideas about the glass ceilings and early suggestions for flooring materials.

The 5500-square-foot Puget Sound house, completed
in 1986, was designed as a weekend and vacation
home for a large extended family of all ages. The first
concept envisaged a straight-line plan resting on a
single plane. The clients suggested a looser arrangement of vernacular forms. The final design comprises
four distinct, linked pavilions: a service pavilion including kitchen and workshops, a formal dining pavilion,
a master bedroom and a main living area looking
towards Mount Rainier. A vaulted swimming pavilion was added in 1999. The pavilions, greenhouses
and a free-standing entrance gate surround a small
courtyard. Children's recreation and guest rooms are
on a lower level. Design team: Nick Milkovich, Inara
Kundzins, Tom Robertson, Kon-Hee Ho.

Asked to include a pitched roof, Erickson related vernacular, modernist and classical motifs. Traditional
rural buildings in the region inspired the cedar-clad
columns, roofs, ceilings and siding. Selected walls of
the house are made with quarried stone, drawing on a
number of North American modernist precedents. The
overall organization draws on the Acropolis in Athens.

Arthur Erickson, Khosla House, Portola Valley, California (1986).

Khosla house frankly draws, suggests that the fluid distances of space and time are best captured not through the vast horizon but from things near at hand, and from lending geometry and enclosure to reflections, sounds and motion, as in water.

It is on the island of Maui, however, in a house completed in 1999, that Erickson's negotiation of infinity takes flight. "His work," wrote critic Peter Blake in 1988, "is a play of spaces as well as forms—with the spaces sometimes extending as far as the eye can see,"[25] and the Maui house is simply a set of floating planes of cantilevered concrete, and of glass and water that draw the sea and sky inside and that draw the eye out to the inchoate elements beyond. With it, ancient traces are abandoned, and everything is devoted to achieving what Erickson called "a penetration of view," uniting the internal recesses of the house to its external spaces, thus gaining "a clear expression of the simultaneity of space and time."[26] To find an example of this difficult idea, Erickson looked back to Le Corbusier's Villa Savoye, and to the simultaneous discoveries of Einstein and the cubists that "every object is only space and that all space is one."[27] With this, we contemplate quite another idea of the infinite, and perhaps are back both in the world of Lawren Harris where Erickson's aesthetic philosophy began, and in a conscious cantilevered homage to Wright, in which architecture set out to dissolve all boundaries between the mystic and scientific, between the space within and the space without.

NOTES

1. Arthur Erickson, "The Weight of Heaven," *Canadian Architect* 9 (1964), 50.
2. Arthur Erickson, *The Architecture of Arthur Erickson* (Montreal and Plattsburgh, NY: Tundra Books, 1975), 33.
3. Erickson, "The Weight of Heaven," 50.
4. Erickson, *The Architecture of Arthur Erickson* (1975), 33.
5. Arthur Erickson, in discussion with the author, 1999–2004.
6. Edith Iglauer, "Profiles: Seven Stones," *New Yorker*, June 4, 1979, 49–50.
7. Erickson, "The Weight of Heaven," 50.
8. Arthur Erickson, *The Architecture of Arthur Erickson* (Vancouver/Toronto: Douglas & McIntyre, 1988), 51.
9. Erickson, in discussion with the author.
10. Ibid.
11. Ibid.
12. Ibid.
13. Ibid.
14. Ibid.
15. Ibid.
16. Arthur Erickson, *Thoughts on Architecture: A Personal View*, unpublished manuscript at the Canadian Centre for Architecture, Montreal, 1999.
17. Erickson, *The Architecture of Arthur Erickson* (1988), 20–21.
18. Erickson, in discussion with the author.
19. Ibid.
20. Ibid.
21. Ibid.
22. Ibid.
23. Erickson, "The Weight of Heaven," 50.
24. Cornelia Hahn Oberlander in conversation with the author, April 2005.
25. Erickson, *The Architecture of Arthur Erickson* (1988), 11.
26. Erickson, *Thoughts on Architecture: A Personal View.*
27. Erickson, in discussion with the author. See also Erickson, *Thoughts on Architecture: A Personal View.*

facing page: Arthur Erickson with Nick Milkovich Architects, Maui house, Hawaii (1999).

The Helmut Eppich House, Vancouver

STAIRS ARE at once sculptural objects, symbolic bridges between realms and a dense site of phenomenological *ekstasis,* literally, astonishment. At the Eppich house, a concrete stair evokes all three categories and simultaneously becomes the synecdoche of these possibilities for the entire house.

The house and its surrounding landscape create a whole where the horizon disappears, blurred by the multilayered horizontal elements in the building. The photographs reveal a strategy utilized in several of Erickson's other projects, both domestic and public. The program is arranged pragmatically, descending the sloped site as garage, bedrooms, living and dining, pool, pond. The house both recedes into the landscape, creating cave-like rooms two storeys underground, and tumbles out through a series of layers of glass walls, terraces and stairs.

The building explores a post-and-beam structural system. A late example of Vancouver modernism, it uses concrete—the first house built by Erickson in this material—rather than the expected rough-sawn fir timber beams. Ancient Greek builders used construction to express the different ways the beams and columns act against the force of gravity, most notably in the play with *entasis*—the apparent bulging out of the column to indicate the force of gravity. Unlike these classical predecessors, the vertical columns and the horizontal beams of the Eppich house have the same dimensions.

Nevertheless, the complex evokes the architecture of the Far East and the Mediterranean, especially places where water is an integral part of the design. For the camera only hints at how at the Eppich house, the reflections of the house and garden in the water, visible both as you stroll around the pond or look out from a terrace, induce a sense of wonder.

Ricardo L. Castro & David Theodore

The University of British Columbia
Museum of Anthropology, Vancouver

. . . .

FOR THE MUSEUM OF ANTHROPOLOGY, Erickson created a "cosmic spatial plot." The architecture tells a story about the museum's place in the universe of human cultural experience (anthropology writ large), grounded in local stories—colonialism, First Nations history, the particularities of Point Grey and the university community—and transmitted in time as visitors tread the pathways of the museum.

The Museum of Anthropology sits on Point Grey overlooking English Bay at the entrance to Vancouver's harbour. It is positioned between the ruins of concrete mounts for three six-inch guns, installed during the Second World War. The university demolished one concrete mount in 1973; a second is now a memorial outside the museum, camouflaged by landscaped topography; the third forms the base for a monumental sculpture *Raven and the First Men,* carved from laminated yellow cedar by the Haida artist Bill Reid.

Such a strong built remnant of the regional response to global events would be enough to anchor the project. But the museum assimilates three additional cultural architectural references as easily as the gun emplacements: the Acropolis in Athens, a Japanese Shinto sanctuary and the re-creation of a Haida village—all of which are manifested, too, in Cornelia Hahn Oberlander's landscape design.

The Greek acropolis forms a key organizational image for the *topothesia*—the thoughtful placement of buildings on the topography and its landscape—of the museum. Indeed, a concrete torii marks the entrance to the museum and the beginning of the visitor's promenade. The repetition of the monumental concrete post and lintel frames evokes the multiple torii that create a continuous tunnel-like structure that unfolds through a Shinto sanctuary. The formal arrangement of the concrete frames is also reminiscent of traditional Haida wooden house frames.

Erickson follows modernist precedents in re-imagining the functional program as *the* generator of form. But he also masks and disguises the tectonic: the reading of the structure and construction of the building. The post and lintel forms in the Great Hall, for example, do not actually function structurally the same way that they do visually. Erickson choreographs the majestic totem poles themselves so that their gazes focus on different spatial points, his interpretation of the placement of the caryatids on the Athenian Acropolis. The fully glazed Great Hall looks out towards the (now dry) reflecting pool and, in the distance, the sea.

Ricardo L. Castro & David Theodore

The Bagley Wright House, Seattle

THE BAGLEY WRIGHT HOUSE longs for the sea: it is oriented towards distant views of Puget Sound. Indeed, the house establishes links with many places and ideas distant in time and space. The doubled concrete columns recall classical Palladian ideals, filtered through beaux-arts neo-classicism and executed with the precise luxury of Mies van der Rohe's postwar houses. Yet, they also are variants of the torii, a form that often appears in Erickson's work.

For the visitor, though, first impressions are dominated by two strong archetypes: the walled gated garden and the clearing in the woods. The huge clearing is artificial, the felled trees replaced by Cornelia Hahn Oberlander with plantings of primal wildflowers. But the overall planning is axial: the edges of the site are clearly defined, and the house's symmetrical arrangement of columns continues into the outdoor reflecting and swimming pools. The tamed and melancholy combination of building and landscape evokes Japanese complexes such as the Katsura Villa in Kyoto: silence is eloquent.

Inside, the planning balances the exigencies of domestic privacy with a mandate to display the owners' prodigious collection of modern and contemporary art, with mixed success—sometimes the art seems to compete with the architecture.

Photographers will note that the house works as a viewing device. The glass canopy that runs transversally on the roof organizes a view of the surrounding treetops and the sky, while the axial layering of interior spaces helps frame, in a scenographic fashion, the distant views of the forest to the east and Puget Sound to the west.

The pools, places of repose that reflect both the region's grey light and its watery climate, anchor the house to its site in an act of *topothesia*.

Ricardo L. Castro & David Theodore

The Puget Sound House, Washington

MODERNIST DESIGN is often imagined as a break with the past, a composition of abstract, pure volumes and planes. The Puget Sound house demonstrates a different modernist lineage, that of historical eclecticism. The plan, a group of pavilions organized around a simple courtyard, recalls the traditional layout of rural buildings. Even the entrance is separated as a pavilion.

In designing this rural retreat, Arthur Erickson placed an unusual emphasis on how the building looks, especially the image presented by its facade, instead of the integration with the site or the primacy of the promenade. Still, the promenade—the path visitors weave through the building—is a leading theme. Indoors, hallways, stairs and a ramp connect the various pavilions of the house, meandering through the whole structure, beginning from the arrival pavilion, passing through the communal and utilitarian areas, then reaching to the private quarters and beyond to the axial lap pool and the paths that criss-cross the surrounding gardens.

The living area and the swimming pool pavilions are the pièces de résistance. As in the Bagley Wright House, the living area is a grand viewing device that locates the visitor inside the house in relation with the natural landscapes: the close (the garden), the intermediate (the lake) and the distant (Mount Rainier). The lap pool pavilion, a long rectangle, is the culmination of the interior promenade on its north side, opening into the landscape through an immense round opening carved into the end concrete wall.

Despite this careful articulation of the house's position in the landscape, the classical forms and imagery seem at odds with the visitor's experience, as the photographs show. Why make a neo-Palladian villa in the Pacific Northwest? The house repeats the irony of the Jeffersonian tradition that uses European, aristocratic and Palladian ideals to symbolize enlightened, democratic rural America. The Puget Sound house is a strange, breathless moment of historical eclecticism: the longing to communicate deep historical and topographical meanings tumbles into postmodern silence.

Ricardo L. Castro & David Theodore

LAURENT STALDER · TRANSLATED BY STEVEN WATT

Europe-America-Japan:
In Search of a New Architectural Language

N 1964 AND 1966, Arthur Erickson published two articles on the subject of Japan in *Canadian Architect:* "The Weight of Heaven" and "A Tendency towards Formalism: The Roots."[1] Written following his first trip to Asia in 1961 and after his first practical experience as an architect, later described by Erickson as an "evolutionary period of my career,"[2] these two articles appear to mark a turning point in his work, especially in light of his rare theoretical contributions. "The Roots," which took a broader cultural perspective, carefully compared the different architectural conceptions prevalent in the West and the East. Linking these conceptions to divergent cultural outlooks, Erickson contrasted the tradition of permanent change in Western architecture to the seemingly unbroken tradition of permanence despite change in Japan. The approach undertaken in "The Weight of Heaven" was more focussed, with Erickson analyzing history to deduce rules for his own architectural practice. In this case, Japanese architecture was studied not only as an expression of a living cultural tradition but primarily as the model for a full-fledged formal language, something that modern Western architecture seemed sorely to lack.

At first glance, neither the themes developed nor the goals laid out in the two articles appear particularly original. The traditional Japanese house had been studied since the 1870s in numerous European and American publications, and it had been a source of inspiration for American architects since the 1880s.[3] It was definitively recognized as an influential form for modern architecture in 1953, when it appeared as the third *House in the Garden* in the courtyard of the Museum of Modern Art in New York, following the Marcel Breuer House (1949) and the Gregory Ain House (1950). The Japanese house's "unique relevance to modern Western architecture," and the way its characteristics strangely evoked those still used in codifying modern architecture—"post and lintel skeleton frame construction; flexibility of plan; close relation of indoor and outdoor areas; and the decorative use of structural elements"[4]—only served to further justify the comparison.

Even if its author was following a well-established tradition, "The Roots" nevertheless rejected a purely formal reading of Japan as it had been "sentimentalized by so many Western observers." By contrast, Erickson stressed the "consistency in Japan [which] has to do with inner nature and not outward appearance."[5] He consequently built his arguments by comparing and contrasting the cultural conditions prevalent in Japan and the West in the light of several factors, which notably included religion (the "organic" nature of Taoist philosophy as opposed to the more "mechanical" Christian civilization), social conditions (the "tradition of family" versus "self-determination"), aesthetic considerations (the "perpetuation of the idea" versus the "idea of beauty") and even technical approaches ("craft" versus the "mass-product"),

59

that these two principles—one of dionysic vitality and the other of rational harmony — interlace through Japanese history, the primitive life here nourishing the more ample order of the other.

This parallels perhaps the Apollonian and Dionysic tendencies in Western art, except that the classical in Japan is more refined and its counterpart more violent. In the midst of the controlled equilibrium of Ryo-anri conduct is the unbridled energy of the Shinto festivals; in the confined space of small garden, the unleashed tumult of rocks; in the midst of utter control, untrammelled freedom. The juxtaposition of constraint and freedom in the same work of art creates a poignant tension that infuses the greatest art of Japan.

But the most important and mystifying aspect of Japanese architecture stems from a more direct translation from nature. Nature, guiding behaviour, established also the canons of proportion and composition that differentiate the architecture most distinctively from the west.

The mystery of the architecture confounds anyone trained in the Western way of seeing. In my own case, a month of dilemma and frustration was resolved only when I determined to not leave the garden of the Kokuferu and its seemingly over-precious intalsco until it made sense to me. A morning was passed philosophically but fruitlessly in a shelter overlooking the lake until suddenly a speed of gardeners appeared, pruning the trees and raking the moss. Watching them, the dilemma was resolved. For it became obvious that only a people with a profound understanding of the forms of plants, unfalterable to us, could prune and groom full-size trees with small scissors and make them appear more natural than before. So our aesthetic vision was dominated by the human form, theirs was by plant form.

Western culture developed in cities and so did its architecture. Early in Western history, the wooden prototypes of temples were transformed for permanence and eminence into stone. The sculptors, rather than the carpenters, gave them their final form, determined their proportions, and endowed them with plastic vigour. The urban culture of the West was egocentric — man was the object of philosophic poetry, painting and sculpture. The sculptor, in carving out the temple, reflected the

physical attributes and proportions of the human body. The Greek column had the vigour or grace of the male or female, stood on a foot or pedestal, and supported with a head or capital.

The human form is symmetrical and its vitality comes from an inner physical tension — that of the athlete about to spring. A building can be arranged, therefore, symmetrically, statically but containing the energy of contained motion. The vitality of Western architecture as physical, its forms anthropomorphic. A building indicates the role it plays with human attributes, such as strength, grace, triviality, nobility.

In Japan, the case was different. The human form was not idealized in their art — the nude never because the pre-occupation of the artist. Nature, instead, was the model and into the wooden frame of the building, the architect introduced the forms of nature as the human figure had entered the architecture of the West.

The plant form has no such attribute as muscular tension, but reaches out asymmetrically on a line of growth and achieves its vitality in the rhythm, the grace and the infinite extension of the growth line. Such rhythm and asymmetrical balance is characteristic of Japanese structure.

In Japan the tree is pruned to have a kind of freely unfolding rhythm that expands and reaches outwards in a manner measured by the kind of tree. Nature requires incompleteness as a condition of growth. Thus a branch emerges strongly from the stem of a tree and gradually dissolves in size creating a line that continues beyond the end of the branch, finishing somewhere invisible in space. The composition of a vase of flowers, or an arrangement of rocks, carries the same line — incomplete — asserted as if it were in total air — but pointing to its virtual completion in space. Even the Japanese vase suggests this rhythm in a slightly asymmetrical body and the incompleteness of an unfinished lip. The tension in Japanese art is not muscular tension but the tension of an unfinished projection into space.

In the structure of the Japanese house, and particularly the teahouse, there is a studied asymmetry of wall materials, an adaptation of the broken line of the branch where horizontal and vertical members meet. Then a gentle movement, a growth line, is created on the whole facade, line is it the free-dimensional non-plastic but planar composition of the painter.

38 The Canadian Architect December, 1966

Opposite page, bottom: Gardspace near Ova. Above: Shiroishi near Kyoto. Below, left and right: Gardspace near Ova.

THE WRIGHT OF HEAVEN

Maekawa's Tokyo Metropolitan Festival Hall, with its upswept eaves (below) shows the classical lines of the temple and of such buildings as the Golden Pavilion in Kyoto (opposite page). Tange's Kurashiki City Hall (right) recalls Michelangelo and Le Corbusier, but is still based on old Japan — the massive wall of the storehouse or castle.

etc. This conceptual reading pointed to a series of specific architectural responses: "canons of proportion and compositions" found in nature for Japan versus the "proportions of the human body" in Western architecture; a "system of measures" that "relates the members aesthetically" versus "plastic unity" and "structural logic"; "forms of nature" as interpreted by the "carpenter" versus the "human form" of the "sculptor"; "asymmetry" versus "symmetry"; a "gentle shifting manner" linking interior and exterior space versus dimensions determined by the "human path," etc. Thus, through this enumeration of dichotomies, emphasis was placed primarily on the fundamental distinctions between the two cultures, while architectural arguments developed out of the observed differences. Summing up his observations, Erickson concluded the article by noting: "From Japanese architecture there is much that is unique for us to learn: the range of feeling, the manner of composition, the sensitivity to materials, the awareness of surroundings."[6]

Indeed, while recognizing the importance of Japanese architecture for his own practice, and even despite the fact that Erickson's first projects after returning to Vancouver clearly showed formal Japanese influences—such as the rough stone foundations of the Baldwin house, the interplay between dark wood structure and white panels in the second Smith house, or the screen with a circular opening that framed the view from the first Eppich house—Japanese architecture was principally portrayed as the accomplished formal expression of a practice solidly anchored in an authentic and apparently purely insular culture. It seemed to offer a clear reflection of a society as much as it did of specific geographic conditions.

However, as Erickson explained in "The Weight of Heaven," it was not a matter of presupposing a "regionalism… due to heritage, technique or race," but instead of finding a "meaning… due to climate and terrain." Thus, the Japanese temples, whose roofs expressed the "weight of heaven," were as much a result of such a meaning as their Greek counterparts, described as "a jewel, flattering the earth"; the Gothic cathedrals, whose spires seemed "to draw the whole village in its wake to reach the sky"; the French palace, capable of imposing its "patterns for miles about on nature and town alike," or even the architecture of Frank Lloyd Wright, which reflected his "love of nature."[7] The argument was, therefore, twofold: on the one hand, architecture was an expression of particular social and natural conditions—climate, season, flora, colour, and especially light and location; on the other hand, architecture transcended cultural differences in order to express general and immutable principles.

These various examples were drawn from observations that Erickson made during his "Grand Tour" of Europe and the Middle East, undertaken between 1950 and 1952, as well as during his trip to Japan in 1961. They also bore witness to an increased interest in the field of world architectural history as popularized by such series as *The Pelican History of Art*[8] and McGraw-Hill's *World Architecture*.[9] Beyond their cultural distinctiveness, the examples were the expression of a structural approach to architecture whose aim was to seek out a universal language, an outlook free of historical constraints, which began to grow in popularity during the inter-war period with writings like Le Corbusier's *Vers une Architecture* and which found its most radical expression in 1964 with the publication of architect Bernard Rudofsky's *Architecture with-*

out Architects.[10] While presenting his arguments in a decidedly conventional fashion—beginning with questions of urbanism, such as the site, urban form and public spaces; then, after some passing remarks on industrial architecture, discussing different architectural elements, such as pilings, towers, walls and roofs—the work was a veritable treatise on world architecture. It was as much an illustration of cultural differences through the juxtaposition of examples as it was a study of the "spontaneous and continuing activity of a whole people with a common heritage."[11]

Not only did Erickson make extensive use of *Architecture without Architects* to illustrate his 1965 publication, *Habitation: Space, Dilemma and Design*,[12] but the same synchronic reading also characterizes the description of his own projects: in terms of the site, as with the Graham house's "play on water," inspired by the Villa d'Este, or the Baldwin house, whose relationship to water evoked the "lake palaces of Moghul India"; in terms of the form, as with the Catton house, whose volumetrics drew on those of "Swiss farmhouses"; in terms of the structure, as with the Smith house, whose rough appearance evoked the "log cabin"; or in terms of the materials, as with the Hilborn house, whose bricks reflected "the traditional building material of the area."[13] More immediate—thereby underscoring the permanence of cultural conditions—were the references to West Coast architecture, such as the log structure of the Boz Scaggs house project on Lasqueti Island, which echoed Kwakwa̲ka'wakw architecture, the arches of the University of British Columbia Museum of Anthropology, which evoked in equal measure both the torii of a Japanese

facing page, top: Page layout from Erickson's essay "A Tendency towards Formalism: The Roots," published in *Canadian Architect* 11 (December 1966), pp. 28–36.

facing page, bottom: Two-page layout from Erickson's essay "The Weight of Heaven," published in *Canadian Architect* 9 (March 1964), pp. 48–53.

temple and the front entrance of Kwakw<u>aka</u>'wakw houses, or even the landscaping of the museum's grounds by Cornelia Hahn Oberlander, simulating "the Haida country from the Queen Charlotte Islands."[14] These examples are particularly revealing. In fact, beyond the references noted above, they were as much the expression of a systematic reading with an eye to defining a "kind of accommodation in the broadest terms of use, meaning, context and time," as they were a reflection of a specific architectural "relationship with the environment—general, particular, past, present, natural, and man-made."[15]

Furthermore, this systematic approach was reflected as much in the phenomenological reading of the location as in the clarity of the architectural bias, in the geometric language and even in the methods of composition. Thus, the approach was evident in the distinctions drawn between different kinds of sites—"meadow, vale, forest, hillside, cliff face, lakeshore" and "clearing"[16]—and between different lighting environments—"hard and glaring, or ineffably soft and luminous."[17] It could also be seen in the thematization of different structural systems: cantilevered shells (Thompson house project), skeleton construction (Smith house), framework structures (Hassard house project), or simply wall panels (Hilborn house). It is also visible in the structural use of the building materials: brick walls or concrete pillars with exposed wooden beams (Craig house), wood and stone panels framed in concrete (Eppich house I and Bagley Wright house), wood posts with plaster panels (Smith house) or even steel frames with glass panels (Eppich house II). It was further evident in the distribution of served and servant spaces, which were distinguished by their volumes (Craig house), by their structural elements (Eppich I) or by their spatial organization (Bagley Wright house). Likewise, it can be seen in the simplicity of the geometric vocabulary: volume (Puget Sound house), plan (Hilborn house) and point (Eppich I). And finally, it is evident in the clarity of the rules of composition: linear (Bagley Wright house) or concentric addition (Smith house II), division (Catton house) and superimposition (Graham house).

This approach, liberated as it was from "preconceived formal sets" and seeking the "essence of materials light, line, plane and volume," corresponded to the pedagogical principles inherited from Bauhaus, as summarized by Erickson and diffused in North America by such individuals as László Moholy-Nagy, Gyorgy Kepes and Gordon Webber.[18] The "mastery of the tool" was nevertheless not sufficient. Much more generally, and following the Japanese example, it was necessary to develop a "language" of architecture capable of expressing the "mood and states of feeling" of the site and its inhabitants. The words chosen by Erickson were evocative. Notably, "mood" and "feeling" were the terms repeatedly used by the "West Coast Painters," especially Lawren Harris, to describe a direct and sensual relationship with nature.[19] Similarly, a few years later, while searching for that same unity, Richard Neutra, whose architecture was considered in Vancouver as a model for the "west-coast,"[20] developed in *Mysteries and Realities of the Site* a more scientific and somewhat psychological approach as an alternative to "primitive animism." In particular, he proposed that the landscape be understood not only as a "physical" or "physiological form," but also as a "physiognomic phenomenon of mental significance and content," to which the architect, through his building, had to give "human responses," such as "view," "exposure" and "privacy."[21]

Likewise using the metaphor of human language, Erickson spoke of the need to recognize the specific—if "sometimes obscure"—qualities of a site by an "act of recognition," allowing for the establishment of a " 'dialogue' between a

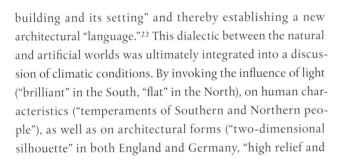

Photos from Erickson's pamphlet *Habitation: Space, Dilemma and Design* (1966), pp. 7, 13.

building and its setting" and thereby establishing a new architectural "language."[22] This dialectic between the natural and artificial worlds was ultimately integrated into a discussion of climatic conditions. By invoking the influence of light ("brilliant" in the South, "flat" in the North), on human characteristics ("temperaments of Southern and Northern people"), as well as on architectural forms ("two-dimensional silhouette" in both England and Germany, "high relief and

deep volume in Italy"),[23] Erickson definitively abolished the boundaries, both symbolic and physical, between architecture, nature and human beings; between interior and exterior, and between interiority and exteriority. In practice, artificial and natural elements would be similarly reabsorbed into a "structural approach to landscape and a landscape approach to architecture."[24]

"Mood" is also the term repeatedly used by Japanese architect Kenzo Tange in his foreword to *Katsura*, cited at length by Erickson in "The Roots" to describe the "spiritual unity" of the villa, which was portrayed as a reflection of a "personal experience or emotion," and of the original Japanese creative force. Formalized within an ongoing tradition, it found its architectural expression in a "sense of perspective, of continuity, of counterpoint."[25] "The rhythm of the growth line," "the gesture towards the infinite," and "the most fragile of moods" were the expressions employed by Erickson to similarly describe the characteristics of Japanese architecture as embodied in the Katsura Villa and its garden. As a reflection of religious conditions —"Zen conception"—as well as social ones—"clash of Jomon [plebeian vitality] with Yayoi [aristocratic serenity]"[26]—the architectural language ultimately found its fulfillment as a symbolic form.

This understanding of architecture as the expression of cultural forces also dominates Erickson's unpublished memoirs of his voyage to Europe and the Middle East, whose architecture he describes first of all as an expression of different tensions: social forces (the Hagia Sophia "vibrant with Christian tension"), aesthetic impressions (the Parthenon, a balance between "horizontal and vertical visual energy"), acoustic sensation (the Place St. Pierre, whose "vastness" could be measured only "through the sound" of Christmas hymns), spatial relations (the Place St. Marc and the Piazzetta, representing a dynamic unity and expressing the difficulty of bringing "into harmony disparate elements") or even intellectual considerations (the paintings of Fra Angelico, Giotto and Massacio, each "a revelation of a new spirit").[27] Once again, the differences between the various examples were absorbed into a single, dynamic and all-encompassing vision of culture.

The same approach had been formulated, beginning in the 1930s, in the theoretical works of László Moholy-Nagy, Alexander Dorner and Gyorgy Kepes. "Spatial forces," "internal forces," "similarity or equality," "continuance" and "closure," "rhythm" and "spatial progression" were some of the basic categories of "plastic organization" developed by Kepes in *Language of Vision*, building on the theories of the "Gestalt psychologists." An expression of a new "symbolic order of

his [man's] psychological and intellectual experiences," with its own "dynamic iconography," it provided a concise summary of the modern holistic project. Its goal was a "new vital structure-order, a new form on a social plane," corresponding to "present knowledge and technological possessions."[28] These same aesthetic categories are also present in Erickson's projects, whether in the multiplicity of points of view (Hilborn house) or in the interplay between transparency and opacity (Smith house II), between physical unity and openness to the infinite (Bagley Wright house), between repetition and progression (Museum of Anthropology), or between harmony and tension (Eppich house I).[29] These categories were as much a reflection of the new modern language of art as developed by Kepes as of the demands formulated by Erickson in "The Weight of Heaven," where they were treated as the basis of a new architectural language, whose forms would once again serve as contemporary "symbols, like words, units of meaning that, put together, make sense out of previous confusion."[30]

Beyond the convergence of artistic theory and architectural practice, these examples also illustrate the direct links between artistic theory and historical analysis. In fact, the "asymmetry of the facades," the "balance of textures" and the "broken planes and incomplete lines" were also all characteristics of Japanese architecture as observed by Erickson in the Katsura Villa.[31] This particular example is not without deeper significance. For example, the noted designer Christopher Dresser, who offered a detailed description of his visit to Kyoto, does not even mention Katsura in his 1882 book on Japanese decorative arts. This absence also marks Edward Morse's first study of Japanese architecture, which dates from

1886. And in his 1905 monograph on Japanese architecture, Ralph Adams Cram devoted less than half a page to it. The first extensive treatment of the Katsura Villa in a Western publication was by architect Yoshida Tetsuro in 1935, but it was not until 1937 that the villa became, through architect Bruno Taut's writings, an icon of modern architecture.[32] The historical analysis was therefore not just limited to the observation of cultural differences. More broadly, it also represented the search for a new cultural and artistic unit, the content of which changed according to the approach taken.

However, the method and the goal remained the same. Indeed, looking beyond its temporal and thematic specificity, the discourse on Japan was itself the manifestation of a Western cultural tradition. Thus, the various categories contrasted in Erickson's two articles—Buddhism and Christianity, cultural tradition and the progress of civilization, nature and culture, form and function, craftsmanship and mass production—had been recurring themes in the literature since the late nineteenth century.[33]

As early as 1882, Christopher Dresser observed that, in contrast to the English, "the Japanese have never been great Engineers, but they have, undoubtedly, been great architects."[34] Ralph Adams Cram noted in 1905 that "all the art of Europe is individual: all the art of the East is communal."[35] Again, in 1937, Bruno Taut situated the foundations of European culture in "Greek logic" and those of Eastern culture in "Asiatic universality."[36] A few years later, Walter Gropius spoke in terms of the "restlessness to capture new horizons" and the "spiritual intensification from the Oriental mind."[37] In 1966, Erickson contrasted in the same way "western humanism" to a certain "formalism" characteristic of Japanese architecture.[38]

Another recurring feature of this literature is the synthesis suggested by its historical reading of architecture. By trac-

ing the origins of the Eastern and Western traditions back to their common source, the "style of Greece," Cram predicted, through his ethnographic reading of architecture, an eventual cultural renewal "between East and West," thereby implicitly suggesting the geographic location of the meeting place: America.[39] Frank Lloyd Wright[40] had been more straightforward in linking the origins of the new organic American architecture to a rejection of English influences, combined with the philosophical influences of Lao Tse: "of nature, for Nature."[41] And again in 1955, Sigfried Giedion observed, in the Japanese edition of his widely read study *Space, Time and Architecture,* that "Western civilization is itself actually in a stage of transition," leading "toward a new hybrid development—a cross between Western and Eastern civilizations." It was in this locus of spiritual encounter that Giedion transposed the main argument of his book, namely the fundamental unity of "thinking and feeling," of technology and architecture, replacing the opposition between East and West within a dualism firmly grounded in the German idealist tradition.[42] Erickson similarly stated in "The Roots" that "each of us could do with something of the other,"[43] concluding a few years later: "I am fortunate that I can stand in Canada, a country without a culture, and look at the world."[44]

Ultimately, it is precisely in this double ambiguity between history and artistic theory on the one hand ("The Weight of Heaven")—and between history and architecture on the other hand ("The Roots")—that the historical analysis and architectural production favoured by Erickson and his predecessors found their meanings, through the structural and contemporary dimensions of the former and through the cultural and historical dimensions of the latter.

NOTES

1. Arthur Erickson, "The Weight of Heaven," *Canadian Architect* 9 (March 1964), 48–53; Arthur Erickson, "A Tendency towards Formalism: The Roots," *Canadian Architect* 11 (December 1966), 28–36.

   On the influence of Japanese architecture in Canada, which seems to have been very weak before the 1950s, see *RAIC Journal* 8 (1955), 272–99. For Vancouver, Douglas Shadbolt mentions certain Japanese influences in the work of Ron Thom and Fred Hollingsworth, beginning in the 1950s ("wood sliding doors," "shoji screens," "lanterns"), influences transmitted through American architect Harwell Hamilton Harris. See *Vancouver Art and Artists, 1931–1983* (Vancouver: Vancouver Art Gallery, 1983), 111; see also: Michael J. McMordie, "Modern Architecture," *Canadian Architect* 29 (March 1984), 22–27, especially 25.

2. Arthur Erickson, *The Architecture of Arthur Erickson* (Vancouver/ Toronto: Douglas & McIntyre and London: Thames & Hudson, 1988), 27. This formative period lasted until around 1963.

3. On the influence of Japanese architecture on North American architectural production, see Clay Lancaster, *The Japanese Influence in America* (New York: Walton H. Rawls, 1963). Frank Lloyd Wright's affinity for Japanese architecture is particularly well documented. See Kevin Nute, *Frank Lloyd Wright and Japan: The Role of Traditional Japanese Art and Architecture in the Work of Frank Lloyd Wright* (New York: Van Nostrand Reinhold, 1993); Julia Meech-Pekarik, *Frank Lloyd Wright and the Art of Japan: The Architect's Other Passion* (New York: Japan Society and Harry N. Abrams, 2001).

4. Arthur Drexler, *The Architecture of Japan* (New York: Museum of Modern Art and Arno Press, 1955), 262.

5. Erickson, "A Tendency towards Formalism: The Roots," 28.

6. Ibid., 36.

7. Erickson, "The Weight of Heaven," 50.

8. *The Pelican History of Art,* Nikolaus Pevsner, ed. (Harmondsworth: Penguin Books, 1953–1969). In 1947, Erickson referred to two "Penguin Books," one on Europe, the other on Japan. The first undoubtedly corresponds to Nikolaus Pevsner, *An Outline of European Architecture* (Harmondsworth: Penguin Books, 1943). However, there does not appear to have been a Penguin Books publication on the subject of Japan before the study by Robert Treat Paine and Alexander Soper, *The Art and Architecture of Japan* (Harmondsworth: Penguin Books, 1955). See the letter from Arthur Erickson to Mrs. Leslie, March 12, 1947, in the Arthur Erickson archives at the Canadian Centre for Architecture, Montreal.

9. *World Architecture: An Illustrated History* (New York: McGraw-Hill, 1963).

10. Bernard Rudofsky, *Architecture Without Architects: A Short Introduction to Non-pedigreed Architecture* (Garden City, NY: Doubleday, 1964). This debate was also carried on in the American journals of the period: Pietro Belluschi, "The Meaning of Regionalism in Architecture," *Architectural Record* 118 (December 1955), 131–39; Paul Rudolph, "The Six Determinants of Architectural Form," *Architectural Record* 120 (October 1956), 183–90; Aldo van Eyck, "Architecture of the Dogon," *Architectural Forum* 115 (September 1961), 116–21, 186.

11. Rudofsky, *Architecture Without Architects,* n.p.

12. Arthur Erickson, *Habitation: Space, Dilemma and Design* (Ottawa: Canadian Housing Design Council, 1965). Most of the illustrations of non-European and non-American cultures were drawn from Rudofsky's publication.

13. Erickson, *The Architecture of Arthur Erickson* (1988), 49, 27, 55, 51, 57.

14. Information graciously provided by Cornelia Hahn Oberlander. Since on-site observations were not possible due to budgetary constraints, she identified, using a magnifying glass, the plants from the illustrations appearing in Anthony Lawrence Carter, *This Is Haida* (Vancouver: privately published, 1968).

15. Erickson, *Habitation,* 5.

16. Arthur Erickson, *The Architecture of Arthur Erickson* (Montreal: Tundra Books, 1975), 23. The category "clearing" is missing from this particular list but was often included in other contexts, such as when discussing the Smith house (81).

17. Erickson, *The Architecture of Arthur Erickson* (1975), 33.

18. Ibid., 18. Erickson studied at McGill under Gordon Webber. Speaking of the "basic design course," Erickson also explicitly mentions Kepes and Móholy-Nagy.

19. Bess Harris and R.G.P. Colgrove, eds., *Lawren Harris* (Toronto: Macmillan of Canada, 1969). David P. Silcox, *The Group of Seven*

and Tom Thomson (Toronto: Firefly Books, 2003). On the subjects of Harris's spiritual sources, including Ralph Waldo Emerson and Henry David Thoreau, as well as the definition of Canada as a "northern nation," see 25–30.

On the subject of Harris's influence on Erickson, see Christopher Thomas, "Reconciling the Universal and the Particular: Arthur Erickson in the 1940s and 1950s," *Society for the Study of Architecture in Canada Bulletin* 21 (June 1996), 36–43, especially 38; Edith Iglauer, *Seven Stones: A Portrait of Arthur Erickson, Architect* (Vancouver: Harbour Publishing and Seattle: University of Washington Press, 1981), 40–42, 48; Erickson, *The Architecture of Arthur Erickson* (1988), 17.

20. In 1946, Richard Neutra spent a week in Vancouver at the invitation of B.C. Binning and Fred Amess, who were members of the *Art in Living Group*. See *Vancouver Art and Artists,* 110; also, Douglas Shadbolt, *Ron Thom: The Shaping of an Architect* (Vancouver: Douglas & McIntyre, 1995), 10. Erickson and Thom met Neutra through Binning. See Harold Kalman, *A History of Canadian Architecture,* vol. II (Toronto: Oxford University Press, 1994), 787.

21. Richard Neutra, *Mysteries and Realities of the Site* (Scarsdale, NY: Morgan & Morgan, 1951), 14, 11–12, 15.

22. Erickson, *The Architecture of Arthur Erickson* (1975), 23.

23. Ibid., 33; Erickson, *The Architecture of Arthur Erickson* (1988), 20–21.

24. Arthur Erickson, *The Architecture of Arthur Erickson* (1975), 14.

25. Kenzo Tange, Foreword to *Katsura: Tradition and Creation in Japanese Architecture* (New Haven, Conn: Yale University Press, 1960), v.

26. Erickson, "A Tendency towards Formalism: The Roots," 35.

27. Erickson, "Chapter V. Hejira," n.p.

28. Gyorgy Kepes, *Language of Vision* (Chicago: P. Theobald, 1944), 14, 12.

29. This debt to Kepes, and even more explicitly to Giedion, is particularly evident in Arthur Erickson, "Speech to McGill University, School of Architecture," lecture, October 21, 2000, McGill University, Montreal.

30. Erickson, "The Weight of Heaven," 48.

31. Erickson, "A Tendency towards Formalism: The Roots" 35.

32. Christopher Dresser, *Japan: Its Architecture, Art, and Art Manufactures* (London: Longmans, Green, and Co., 1882); Edward Sylvester Morse, *Japanese Homes and Their Surroundings* (New York: Harper, 1885); Ralph Adams Cram, *Impressions of Japanese Architecture and the*

Allied Arts (New York: Baker & Taylor, 1905), 60. Yoshida Tetsuro, *Das Japanische Wohnhaus* (Berlin: E. Wasmuth, 1935). Thanks to Taut, this "second Stadtkrone," as he used to call it in his journal, became, after 1937, a true point of reference: Bruno Taut, *Houses and People of Japan* (Tokyo: Sanseido Press, 1958 and 1937), 275–93; also, Manfred Speidel, "Bruno Taut in Japan" in *Ich liebe die Japanische Kultur. Kleine Schriften über Japan* by Bruno Taut and Manfred Speidel (Berlin: Gebrüder Mann, 2003), 7–39.

33. In particular, Erickson refers to Alan W. Watts, *Nature, Man and Woman* (New York: Pantheon Books, 1958). See Erickson, "A Tendency towards Formalism: The Roots," 28. Within the parallel culture movements on the West Coast, Watts was one of the most important interpreters of Zen Buddhism, along with D.T. Suzuki.

34. Dresser, *Japan,* 243.

35. Cram, *Impressions of Japanese Architecture,* 21.

36. Taut, *Houses and People of Japan,* 259.

37. Walter Gropius, "Architecture in Japan," *Perspecta* 3 (1955), 9.

38. Erickson, "A Tendency towards Formalism: The Roots" 36.

39. Cram, *Impressions of Japanese Architecture,* 78–80, 16–17. Cram supports his theory by pointing to certain motifs, such as the "entasis of the columns of the great gate" and the "thin folds and studied calmness of the sculptured drapery of the statues."

40. Frank Lloyd Wright, *An Organic Architecture: The Architecture of Democracy.* The Sir George Watson Lectures of the Sulgrave Manor Board for 1929. (London: Lund Humphries & Co., 1939), 11.

41. Wright, *An Organic Architecture,* 3–4. On page 11, he describes Japanese architecture as "an expression of the feeling for human form."

42. Sigfried Giedion, *Space, Time and Architecture: The Growth of a New Tradition,* trans. into Japanese by Minoru Ota (Tokyo: Maruzen, 1955), Introduction, cited in Sigfried Giedion, *Architecture, You and Me: The Diary of a Development* (Cambridge, MA: Harvard University Press, 1958), 141.

43. Erickson, "A Tendency towards Formalism: The Roots," 36.

44. This idea is expressed by Erickson in many writings about him, and most explicitly in Iglauer, *Seven Stones,* 20.

Enclosure

"Fragments of Utopia"

Arthur Erickson's career changed course with his master plan for the new Simon Fraser University, awarded to Erickson/Massey in a competition in 1963. Set on a high, forested hill at the eastern edge of Vancouver, the project was an experiment in inventing a space, a program and a collaborative approach to design. The four finalists were assigned the design of the enclosed components, but Erickson/Massey had control of their basic material and design choices, and of the design of all interlocking spaces and infrastructure. Erickson worked with Chancellor Gordon Shrum to develop an atmosphere of learning, built on a dissolution of hierarchy and formality, an integration of disciplines, and an emphasis on casual and intimate exchange.

Erickson stepped the connecting spine of the structure upwards, from dark to light, along an open artery, in which a central space at the hub burst open to a broad rectangular covered court that served as a ceremonial plaza, a meeting place, and a point of assembly and crossing. As this progress rose, it distributed covered promenades farther and farther out, towards the quiet cloistered edges, from which academic buildings dropped downhill under shelves of roof pools. The design, entirely of concrete, was dedicated to flow between spaces, activities, departments and ranks, functionally and symbolically designed "to relate knowledge rather than fragment it."[2]

The scheme was deliberately replete with a mix of sources: the University of Salamanca, the Pergamon, Mayan ruins, Hadrian's villa, the quadrangles of Oxford and the rice terraces of Bali. Greek scale and proportion were used to weave a vast form from elements at a human scale, just as the community of learning and the corpus of knowledge is built from intimate patterns of human exchange.

It was a similar shift in scale that generated the scheme. "If you can design a house," Erickson has said, "you can design anything."[3] But once the scope of an independent project widened, he saw a critical shift in its relationship to context. A small structure must compose itself in dialogue with the landscape. A vast compound must draw the logic of its landscape in. Hence, Erickson describes Simon Fraser as "a remote city," an "urban compression"[4] in which everything turns inward so that the spaces within and the glimpses of vista beyond become the critical factors. This is accomplished by adopting a repeating theme as the logic of construction, in which massive horizontal beams on piers or columns organize the mass and orchestrate the vistas. It was a strategy that Erickson adapted in wood at a domestic scale in the tiny Smith house of 1964.

Erickson took this insistent framing to compelling lengths in the great beam structure of his second campus, outside

"The miracle... is in the space between the Parthenon and the other buildings on the Acropolis and not only the structures of the Acropolis itself, but structures on neighbouring hills, the distant mountains, the harbour and even the path of the sun."[1]

ARTHUR ERICKSON

top right: In 1963, working with Geoffrey Massey, Erickson won a competition to design a campus for the new Simon Fraser University on a 1000-acre mountaintop site in Burnaby, British Columbia. Design team: Ken Burroughs, Ron Bain, Bruno Freschi, Rein Raimet, Leo Ehling, Genje Ogawa, Bing Thom, Fred Dalla-Lana, Dan Lazosky. The master plan organized the university around a central axis that follows the ridge of the mountain, climbing from the transportation centre, through the central mall, up to the academic quadrangle. The gymnasium and terraced playing fields are to the left of the transportation centre.

bottom right: The simple linear concept is meant to encourage social mixing. Students and teachers encounter each other daily in both formal and informal settings. Faculty offices are sprinkled among classrooms, laboratories and lecture rooms. The cascading staircases and central mall create interactions on the model of a pedestrian-oriented urban streetscape.

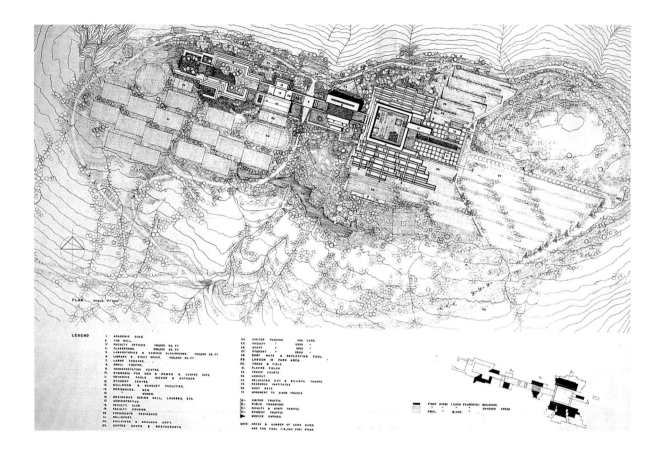

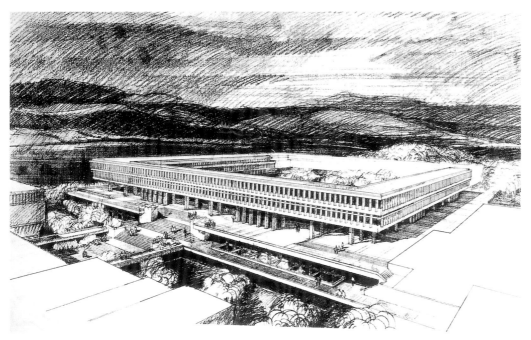

above: Erickson/Massey designed and built the central mall. It connects directly to the library and the theatre. Jeffrey Lindsay engineered the timber and steel space-frame roof, which is covered by a 133-foot by 297-foot glass canopy.

left: In order to finish construction in time for a September 1965 opening, the university gave contracts for portions of the campus to four runners-up in the competition. Zoltan S. Kiss Architects built the academic quadrangle (shown here), following Erickson/Massey's master plan, which called for faculty offices accessible to students and raised above the circulation route, and a perfectly square courtyard bordered by repetitive facades.

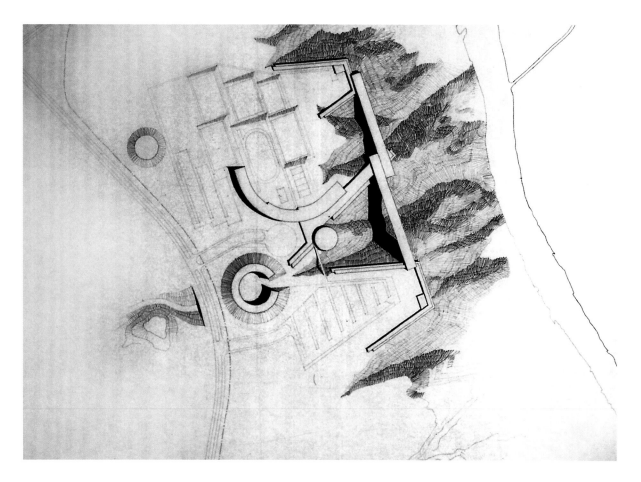

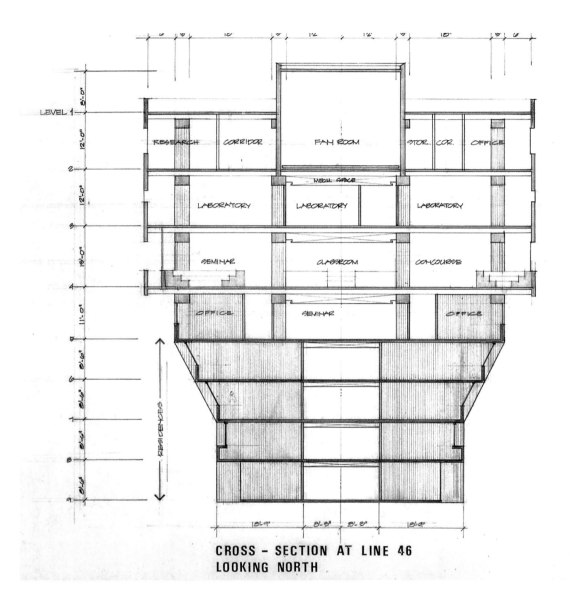

LEVEL 1

RESEARCH | CORRIDOR | FAN ROOM | STOR. | COR. | OFFICE

MECH. SPACE

LABORATORY | LABORATORY | LABORATORY

SEMINAR | CLASSROOM | CONCOURSE

OFFICE | SEMINAR | OFFICE

RESIDENCES

**CROSS - SECTION AT LINE 46
LOOKING NORTH**

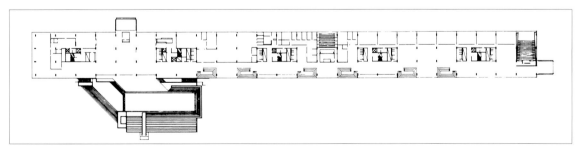

facing page, top: The University of Lethbridge spans a coulee situated across Oldman River from downtown Lethbridge in southern Alberta. Early plans envisioned a two-part building, expanding the university linearly across the prairies. The design echoes the form of the nearby trestle railway bridge and includes a rooftop plaza and vista point. Design team: Ron Bain, Gary Hanson, Rein Raimet, Tad Young, Andy Roost, Byron Olson.

facing page, bottom: Erickson focussed on an iconic, pyramidal program for the two buildings, based on the image of an interior city. The entrance formed a gateway like the portal of a medieval city.

top: The concept of a small city with a concourse level as an inner street demanded multiple sectional studies. Although the final project was scaled back to fit the budget, this early section shows the final concept of a vertical division into laboratories, mid-level concourse and lower-level residences.

bottom: The plan, like the section, was zoned by activity, but meant to facilitate intimate seminar teaching as well as small classes. Students could exit from the concourse onto an outdoor terrace that doubled as a theatre and assembly area.

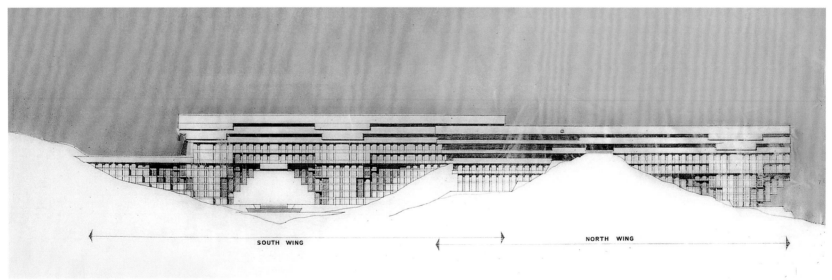

SOUTH WING   NORTH WING

Lethbridge on the Alberta prairie. Erickson/Massey was responsible for the master plan and for all its main components. Two gigantic bridge structures, echoing a trestle bridge nearby, were proposed, but only one was built. Erickson recognized the bridge as "a key source for my design, but not in the way most people think. More than anything else, the High Level Bridge demonstrated to me that the prairies are not flat," but a "shifting topography" of undulating and broken surfaces, in which, as the bridge demonstrated, "an absolute horizontal" would help the eye to see the more fluid and variable contours of the valley as they responded to seasons of light, growth and wind.[5]

In contrast to Simon Fraser University, where he distributed closed spaces into zones of different mood and function with different falls of light, at Lethbridge he compressed activities into one compact structure, in which spaces did double duty and connections became usable rooms. With only the roof of the utility plant available for outdoor space, he took a cue from Le Corbusier and made of it a sculptured concrete playground. Drawing on the Al-Azhar mosque—where he had seen students using the open carpeted floor to gather round a master, to sleep, to talk, to wander or to read—he looked to this interchangeability as cultivating a more "democratic learning environment," a fluid approach to knowledge in which students might "drop in on classes and discussions."[6]

These two signal projects, published internationally as models for the new university movement everywhere, had an extraordinary impact. They are also the first inquiries in a thirty-year laboratory in which Erickson developed propositions for model communities. From the Napp Laboratories near Cambridge (1979–83) to Vancouver's Waterfall (1999–2002), and in a score of essentially unbuilt projects between 1976 and 1985 for Kuwait, Baghdad, the Arabian peninsula, Algiers and North America, Erickson punctuated his work

with explorations of the ideal city. Setting up aesthetic enclosures and proposing ways to cluster or consolidate diverse activities towards a common end, these lofty cultural enterprises stand as the true acropolis of his work. Erickson's utopias set out not to reinvent a society and then inflect the buildings to meet it but to imagine buildings in which people might learn new social patterns or recover old ones, through sensing the "fundaments of social grounding"[7] that the architecture draws upon. The first three fundaments Erickson lists as nature, topography, atmosphere, defining them as the handling of colour, light, air, materiality, vista and perspective, and mood; the fourth is human archetypes, ranging from the arts to ceremonial rites and the mode of "managing the elements of life—water, light, growth."[8]

The third and fourth of these fundaments make his work in the Arab world, even though it is essentially unrealized, of extraordinary importance. There, he slowly learned to surrender "a preconceived sense of form and space," including monumentality, axial composition and symmetry, grasping that Muslim culture was based on "formless exteriors" in which everything was incidental to the enclosed spaces, those static, directionless rooms and courts "speaking only for themselves" that are the utopias of the Middle East.[9] Erickson tried to reinvent them to fit modern functions and materials. Just as Simon Fraser and Lethbridge are structured to provide a vista out and to focus on how spaces are linked or united, so the Middle East projects dissolve or cover their anatomy to open a vista into singular spaces that enclose only themselves.

Erickson describes the Middle Eastern work as his "apotheosis of concrete."[10] Here, he would use concrete not as a rugged substance but as he had seen it in Japan, "treated as

facing page, top: In early designs for the University of Lethbridge, Erickson explored models of simple bridge-like forms and articulated the space between the two horizontal pavilions as a dynamic, monumental public plaza.

facing page, bottom: As the design progressed, Erickson removed one of the horizontal pavilions from the original proposition, and compacted the remaining one. The team tested several versions of the streamlined facades in perspective sketches. The final elevation is governed by a stricter emphasis on horizontality.

if it were a precious material."[11] For the brilliant desert light, he would give the concrete a finished opacity, like sandstone, and smooth its surface to blank it in the sun. Concrete, coldly coloured, rough, pierced, shaped and penetrated, talking of structure and tension, would become concrete as an expanse: quiet, warm, smooth and planar.

These investigations in one culture changed Erickson's work in all of them. An art centre for Red Deer, Alberta, in 1981, transported in brick the blank coloured walls of the Arabian peninsula to equally vivid prairie skies and a similar plane of light-toned ground. His own studio in Los Angeles was organized without hierarchy into a casual suite of Andalusian courts, and his California Plaza project consciously tried to lean the dense Arab wall back to soak up the sunlight of Los Angeles. The symbolic storytelling at the Canadian Chancery took a cue from the literary and philosophical narratives in the culture park of Abu Nuwas and the Saudi Arabian Center for Science and Technology. The Middle Eastern patterns of enclosure, concrete landscape and court settled in Erickson's imagination. They come back spacious and simple at the Tacoma Museum of Glass (like the platform of his technical university in Saudi Arabia), and at once walled and wandering, like his housing plans for Kuwait, in the ideal city within a city at Vancouver's Waterfall.

Nature and topography were both in Erickson's list of "groundings" for the ideal city. Outside Cambridge in England, building for a pioneering science park, he realized a working precinct in which the surrounding reality of the contextual landscape (badly disturbed by a highway) was carefully concealed, but its logic strengthened and drawn into a fabricated natural landscape. He won the competition for Napp pharmaceutical laboratories in 1979 and built it on the idea of a single structural shape repeated to make an endless horizontal line,

introduced ten years before at Lethbridge. But Lethbridge does without an independent landscape in order to clarify what can be seen in the surrounding vistas. Napp incorporates natural and topographical elements right into itself. Its two pavilions are shaped like an early British foss-dyke. They are separated by a broad moat from a grass earthwork that echoes their form. Rather than bridging the land, each arch of the building settles into it so firmly that, like a surveyor's tripod, it makes up the emerging ridgeline of a vast frame that drops below the watery surface to a deep, solid subterranean geometry.

The two interlocking pavilions were originally proposed in bent steel and glass, trimmed in lead. When the client suggested concrete for the structural arches, Erickson developed a special aggregate that could attain lustre, and it is this luminescent character that dominates Napp. Inside, surfaces of steel polished to the highest finish are made more reflective as they are offset by steel brushed to a duller sheen. Lighting, the camber and tone of mirror-coated glass, the light from the water, the hard lustrous floors, the reflections of the moat all give the dim light of the English fens a dancing vitality. The simplicity of Napp disguises a complicated symbolic program. The manipulation of materials and light suggests how natural elements are metamorphosed by mixing, distillation and refinement, which are the business of the company, and there is a parallel reference to the high gothic of King's Chapel in the crossing of light in the lobby ceiling and in the forms of the arch: here Erickson addresses another metamorphosis, speaking of how the British Renaissance took a simple medieval building form, derived from the same language of earthworks as the foss and dyke, and wrought it into the concentrated intensity of a perpendicular nave.[12]

top left: The Napp Laboratories building, designed in 1979, sits in an industrial park near Cambridge, England. Earth from the building excavation was used to create a berm surrounding two linked buildings, one housing administration, manufacturing and laboratories, and the other a warehouse. Revisiting an idea first used for Robson Square, Erickson made the reflecting pool on the building's south side the reservoir for the sprinkler system. Erickson's proposal outlined steel ribs and facing, but the client suggested concrete aggregate for the final design. Design team: Alberto Zennaro, Fred Allin, Pui-To Chau, Peter Clewes, Richard Coombs, Rudy Wallman.

top right: The building has ribs of regularly spaced precast concrete columns filled in with mirror-coated, double-glazed curtain wall that is fixed with structural silicone into aluminum frames—the first time the technique was used in England. The simple linear structure was meant to be easily extended, though Erickson's thumbnail sketches (c. 1988) for a research centre on the site explored quite different volumetric ideas.

bottom: A dramatic three-storey lobby connects the office and manufacturing sections, traversed at all levels by bridges. A visitors' gallery looks into the whole length of the manufacturing area. Although the interiors vary widely according to use and function, on the outside the building's shapes are similar.

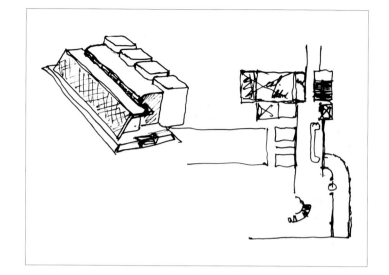

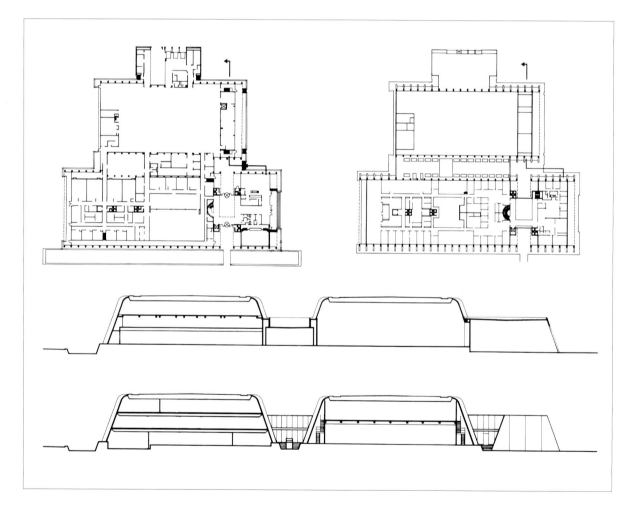

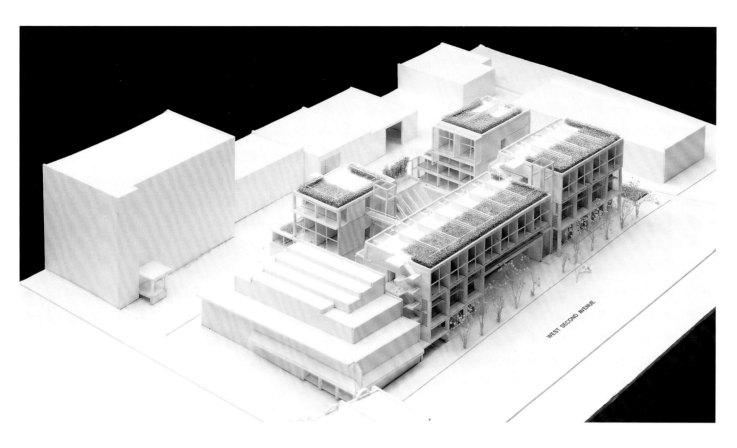

WEST SECOND AVENUE

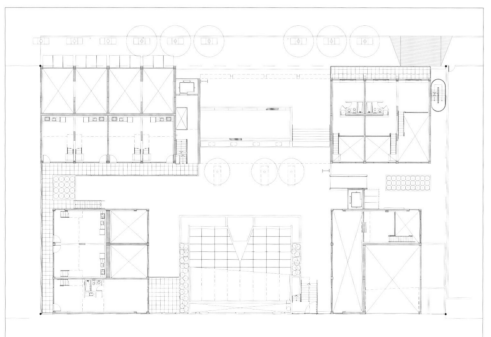

top: The Waterfall Building in Vancouver, British Columbia, organizes five buildings around a communal courtyard planted with grass, cherry trees and white roses. Design team: Nick Milkovich.

bottom: This plan of the ground level shows the central courtyard. A waterfall and reflecting pool animate the entranceway with light and sound. The design seeks to link the open public space of the street and the commercial units that enclose the courtyard.

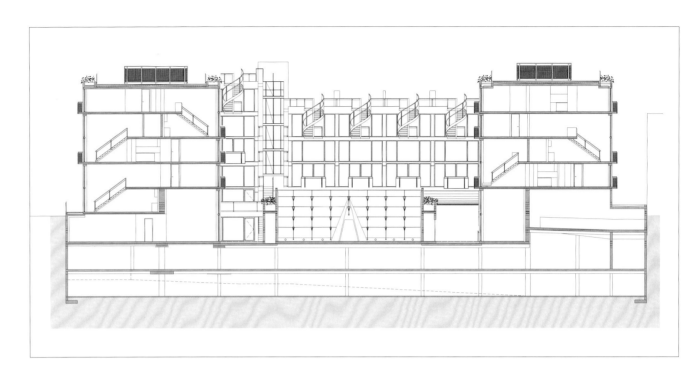

top: Sections show how the Waterfall Building is divided vertically by use: double-height live/work studios on the upper levels, commercial spaces at street level, parking below ground.

bottom: Erickson presented the project as an ideal city. Galvanized-steel spiral staircases, which allow residents to access the roof, however, along with metal railings and screens, enliven the interior courtyard and draw in the disorder of the real city. Waterfall's fundamental symmetry—a sort of hidden ordering device—is manifest only in the section drawing.

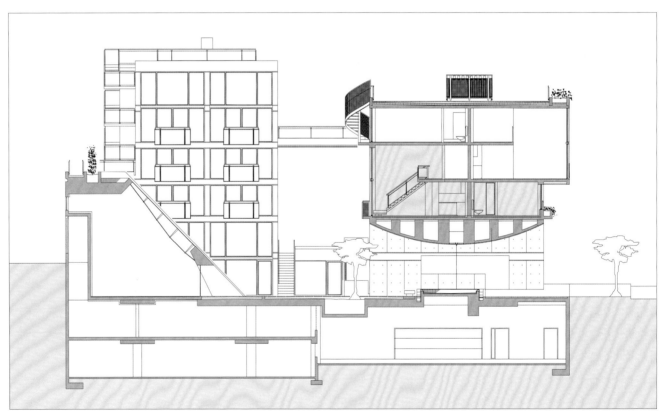

Vancouver's Waterfall—a dense, six-storey complex of living, working, art and commerce—goes back to Erickson's 1960s idea of clustering colonies to make an ideal city. This small project makes a complete cityscape of its own: monument, park, levels and "a sense of bulk, perimeter and scale."[13] A curved concrete beam above its entrance drops a curtain of water like a portcullis, baffling the sound of the streets. An Assyrian pyramid in the centre of the court, again washed with water, gives its public square an open temple. Vista is managed in two ways: every space has a mezzanine level, giving an interior perspective that brings spaciousness inside, and every unit looks two ways. Roof gardens frame the real cityscape to its north, a distant row of stacks of light against the backdrop of dark mountains.

Waterfall, like Napp, takes amorphous surroundings and rearranges their elements inside to create a landscape, not of ordered grassy berms or lawns but of the urban disorder of concrete, steel and glass. There are stairways, mesh screens, walls and doors at every level. Waterfall's developer, Stephen Hynes, sees it as the flagship in his endeavour to "encourage people to co-operate in urban space," remembering that as Hynes was a graduate student in philosophy at Simon Fraser in 1985, "walking along the concourse of the Academic Quadrangle with an armful of books, . . . someone opened a door for him"; when he asked "what would prompt such an act of random kindness. . . his answer came from the layout of the university itself."[14] Thus, one "fragment of utopia"[15] prompted, as it was meant to, the investigation of another.

NOTES

1. Arthur Erickson, *Habitation: Space, Dilemma, and Design*, pamphlet published by Canadian Housing Design Council, Ottawa, 1966, with an appendix, 1967.
2. Arthur Erickson, in discussion with the author, 1999–2004.
3. Ibid.
4. Ibid.
5. Arthur Erickson quoted by Trevor Boddy in "The Design of the University of Lethbridge: Arthur Erickson in His Own Words," in *Lethbridge Modern: Aspects of Architectural Modernism in Lethbridge from 1945–1970*, Gerald Forseth, ed. (Lethbridge: Southern Alberta Art Gallery, 2002), 49.
6. Erickson, in discussion with the author. See also Arthur Erickson, *Thoughts on Architecture: A Personal View*, unpublished manuscript at the Canadian Centre for Architecture, Montreal, 1999 and Erickson quoted by Boddy, 51–52.
7. Erickson, in discussion with the author.
8. Ibid.
9. Ibid. See also Arthur Erickson, unpublished draft of memoirs. Used by permission of the author.
10. Erickson, in discussion with the author.
11. Ibid.
12. Ibid.
13. Ibid.
14. Stephen Hynes, "Arthur Erickson: Vision for a New Order" in *The Social Developer* (Web organ of Hillside Properties, Vancouver, ca. 2002). See also Michael McLaughlin, "The Communitarian Capitalist," *The Republic* (Vancouver), September 16–19, 2004.
15. Erickson, in discussion with the author.

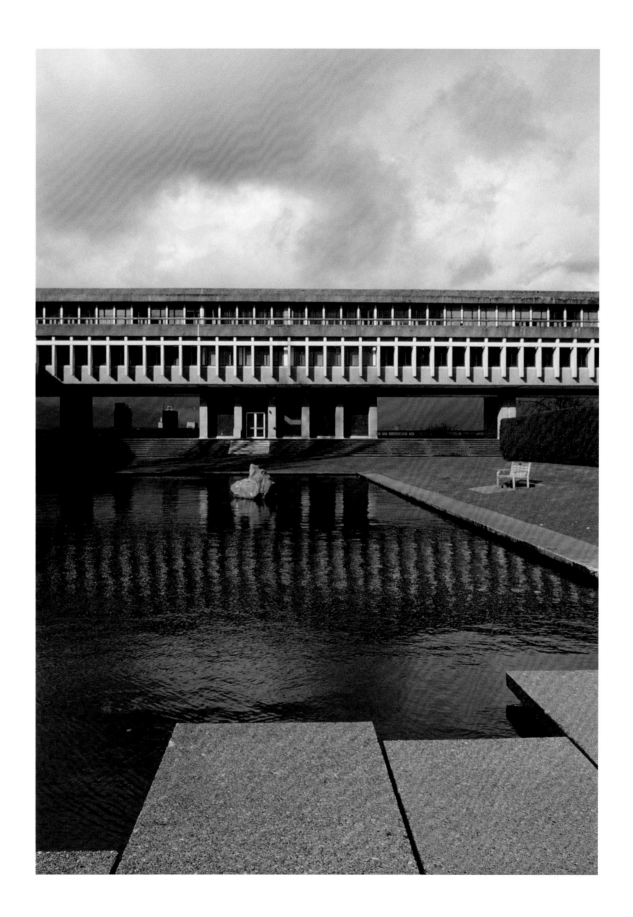

Simon Fraser University, Burnaby

SIMON FRASER UNIVERSITY hides its isolated, mountain location with a (then new) spatiality of academic architecture. It hides its architectural expression as spatial progress rather than iconic identity.

This complex of buildings and courtyards has been compared to a Greek acropolis. It seems, however, to evoke a medieval monastery perched on top of a mountain. A peculiar monastery, nonetheless, since in many instances the surrounding walls are made of arcades open on both sides, allowing a direct connection with the distant landscape. Erickson has not missed here the opportunity of experimenting with *shakkei,* the Japanese concept of borrowing views, which he knows intimately from his studies and travels in the Far East.

But at Simon Fraser University, the photographer is forced to analysis rather than evocation, to analyze the delicate connections of the covering of the mall, the precast concrete walls and the topographical manipulation of the courtyards. The project's sensitivity to joints culminates in the treatment of the walkway architecture made of concrete and clay tiles, accompanied by the flow of water and the spread of grass.

At Simon Fraser University, the camera captures a certain melancholy, expressed not so much as a longing for the distant view, as in Erickson's houses, but rather as a sense that any occupation of a space is temporary: it implies a time and space beyond.

Ricardo L. Castro & David Theodore

85

The University of Lethbridge, Alberta

• • • • • • • • • • • • •

THE DIFFICULTY of photographing the University of Lethbridge lies in the disjuncture between the conceptual strength of the building and the primordial power of the landscape. Recent unsympathetic additions and renovations add complexity to the intricate task of comprehending Erickson's original intention to erect a single unified powerful structure. Like many of Erickson's buildings, it photographs differently according to the weather: lazy and ochre in the summer sun, calm as a boat in its moorings in the autumn and as iconic as the monolith from *2001: A Space Odyssey* in the glare of winter snow.

From a distance, the long form of the building recalls the train bridges familiar from prairie history. Close up, however, the building's power as a megastructure—a self-contained city on stilts—interrupts this feeling of topography and history, replacing it with future-oriented urbanism.

In particular, the university echoes the memorable and ever-present trestle bridge to the north of the campus. The Lethbridge Viaduct, or the High Level Bridge as it is also known, was completed by the Canadian Pacific Railway in 1909. Spanning 1.6 kilometres across the steep banks of the Oldman River, it is the longest and highest bridge (96 metres) of its kind in North America.

Like the viaduct, the phenomenological appearance of Erickson's building—its immaterial yet immensely physical presence—resists the act of reading the landscape. When visitors approach the building from the river, climbing the steep slope of the embankment, the building emerges like a Greek *propylaea*—a gatehouse or porch marking the entrance to a sacred enclosure—perched on an acropolis. The prismatic megastructure, pierced in its centre, acts both as a foil and as a gateway, revealing the depth and shape of the surrounding coulees, and defining a connection between the deep canyon, the grand prairie horizon and the open sky.

Ricardo L. Castro & David Theodore

Napp Laboratories, Cambridge, England

THE NAPP LABORATORIES photograph well under the lazy winter light. Erickson's landscape interventions, which include the planting of rows of hawthorns and poplar against long earth berms, screen the two-block building complex from other facilities in the science park owned by the University of Cambridge. On the one hand, images speak of a futuristic building, something like a spy headquarters for James Bond; on the other hand, the canal that runs along the main building evokes the historic relationship of buildings and water in Cambridgeshire.

A hierarchical organization of space directs the visitor from the parking lot through an outdoor plaza that connects with a bridge that spans the canal and leads to the three-storey reception hall, with furnishings designed by the late Francisco Kripacz. Inside, the corporate symbols of science in industry argue with the ameliorationist spirit of health research.

The building's forms, however, caught in a social mix evocative of Thatcherite Britain, have weathered well both physically and spiritually, taking on the patina of passed optimism and showing how fresh the right materials can stay: concrete, metal and mirrored glass. On the exterior, the camera is drawn to connections: the way the glass and silicone joints promise polish and sheen; the way the bulk of the building and the rolling berms echo distant landscapes—as if research were a matter of digging in the earth, like mining, rather than production and chemical combination, and the way, at night, the building glows like the lights from a distant town.

Ricardo L. Castro & David Theodore

The Waterfall Building, Vancouver

THE IDEA of the courtyard, explored by Erickson in some of his most celebrated projects of the twentieth century, including Simon Fraser University and the Canadian Chancery in Washington, DC, appears once again in Vancouver's Waterfall Building.

One of the architect's most recent commissions in collaboration with Nick Milkovich Architects, the project consists of five separate buildings and a transparent prism that is the focus of the courtyard and was conceived as a gallery and restaurant. The repertory of materials used in this project—concrete, glass, galvanized steel, plant materials and water—are orchestrated in an unorthodox manner that challenges traditional urban dwelling in the Pacific Northwest and celebrates the commercial and industrial past of the area.

A large opening, discreetly obstructed by a hanging basin that feeds a screen of continually falling water, connects the bustling street with this sheltered courtyard. Besides its experiential qualities, the waterfall aids the visual and acoustic separation of these two realms, a separation that the quieter pool and fountains at the prism reinforce.

For the photographer, the large surfaces of glass framed by a smooth concrete structure; the bridges connecting the various sections of the buildings; and the galvanized panels, fixtures and stairs become unique opportunities to engage visually with objects and spaces that inhabit the immediate urban foreground. In the unusual roof gardens, these same elements help to articulate a vision, panoptical as it were, of the middle ground made by the surrounding city fabric, and particularly, in the farther distance, by the tall downtown skyline silhouetted against the magnificent mountainous background.

Ricardo L. Castro & David Theodore

Western Monoliths:
Arthur Erickson's Design for Two Universities

ARTHUR ERICKSON has been variously classified as a West Coast modernist in the school of Richard Neutra, a proponent of Kenneth Frampton's "critical regionalism"[1] and a regional architect in the traditions of Frank Lloyd Wright or Bruce Goff (and Canadian architects who have immersed themselves in their locale, such as Étienne-Joseph Gaboury in Manitoba or Bob Hassel on the Pacific Coast).[2] Although it may be tempting to confuse his work, like Alvar Aalto's, with the landscapes to which it responds, Erickson is much more properly defined as a late modernist of the third or fourth generation. He is, as Peter Blake wrote in 1988, an architect of great originality whose *métier* can trick the senses with a subtle use of light, matter and space, and whose mastery is able to trigger that sense of bafflement and awe that is experienced when entering the central vestibule of the Museum of Anthropology (1973–76) or climbing the stairs of Robson Square (1974–79) in downtown Vancouver, two masterworks that could alone assure him a deserved fame.[3]

In the broader context of Erickson's first experiments in and around Vancouver during the 1950s and the 1960s, it seems clear that the young architect was integrally connected to the fascination with technological innovation and the speculation about scale that marked the progressive thinking of this time. However, his originality consisted of adding to this thinking a search for historical archetypes that, seemingly without contradiction, could be brought within rational, even scientific methods of design—a course that, except for the work of Louis Kahn, few other modernist architects were either inclined to follow or able to achieve. It is this quest—not just to negotiate between past and present but between past precedents and future systems—that is strikingly evident in the two great independent landscapes of the sixties, Erickson's campuses for Simon Fraser and Lethbridge universities.

It is revealing to compare two of Erickson's early texts. In "The Design of a House" (1960),[4] he describes his way of thinking while building elegant residences in the Vancouver area, and in a later one, written with Geoffrey Massey, he centres on the question of museum design (1965).[5] Whereas the first article attempted to give a theory of site and architecture (the term "site" is repeated thirteen times, "space" eleven and "horizon" five), the second, written after winning the competition for Simon Fraser University (1963–65), discussed what constituted the "true essence" of architecture. The second text is crucial to understanding the method used in the conception of SFU. The two designers thought that "most of the traditional solutions for building problems that we still have with us must be re-examined to find that classical type which meets the needs of today, and in being up to the moment in every sense will anticipate the needs for many years to come."

Many sources have been cited *à propos* of Erickson/Massey's winning entry for this new university built on a windy ridge on the eastern outskirts of Vancouver, which aligns on a linear axis such features as student residences to the west, a transportation hub and covered mall in the centre, and an academic quadrangle to the east. Abraham Rogatnick, writing in *The Architectural Review*, became quite lyrical with references: Mount Sinai, Monte Alban, the Parthenon, the Acropolis, Pergamum, the Roman forum and Roman baths, the medieval cloister, Salamanca's Plaza Mayor, Michelange-lo's Laurentian Library, all places that the young architect had visited during his early travels.[6]

Indeed Erickson's travel memoirs, which are based on his diary, possibly nurtured by Friedrich Nietzsche's notion of eternal return, show he was definitely aware of Carl Jung's notion of collective consciousness, note quite precisely the idea of archetypes in reiteration: "We spent the day in Pompeii. I was fascinated by how Pompeii's late society had become much the same as ours, as you could read in the layout of the city and the changing plan of the houses... The baths, the theatre, the stadium, the library were in their likely loca-tions as if the Italian town had never changed... On the out-skirts was the House of the Mysteries—unusual in the larger three-dimensional murals of dramatic figures presumed to be engaged in the Dionysian rites... The spiral of cyclic rep-etition... brings history back to us again and again—near-ing a slightly higher level with each millennial spiral but with the same preoccupations, same evolution of focus from the abstract and spiritual to the idealistic, to physical and materi-alistic pre-occupations..."[7] Erickson himself used the termi-nology of archetypes in his presentation for SFU,[8] and while such thinking could have led him to use formal historical examples in his architectural designs, he was more prudent in his use of references, telling Rogatnick that "few models were in his conscious mind when the design of the complex... was in its formative stage."

If it was not the recollection of historical types that Erick-son wanted to introduce to his method of design, what was it? Perhaps the answer is given by Massey and Erickson them-selves in their discussion of museum planning: "Our think-ing is that the essence of a building is in its section: that a cross-section taken through the building should show every part in its right proportion and relationship, just as a cross-section through the human body shows its basic form and functioning."[9] So the sources for the SFU project are neither Lhasa nor a mortuary temple at Deir el-Bahri in upper Egypt, but an idea primarily expressed by a cross-section through the whole complex, leading from the entrance hub through the agora-mall-*galleria* and reaching the crowning moment of the super-cloister which, though perched on the top of the mountain and at dramatic new scale, recalls the morphology of an Oxbridge quadrangle.

In an appreciation of SFU critically entitled "Architecture of the Indefinite," Vancouver architect Ron J. Thom, designer of the much more intimate quadrangular Massey College in Toronto in 1961, wrote that the SFU buildings appeared "as a crown, inseparable from the top of the mountain."[10] It might be said that the whole complex recalls Bruno Taut's notion of "alpine architecture" (1919), a socialist, utopian vision of glass constructions, recalling the purity of rocks and glaciers in the mountains, and alluding to idealistic ideas of redemp-tion in a period in which the law of gravity seemed to have no bearing.[11] It might also be said that SFU is connected to Taut's idea of "the crown of the city" (1919),[12] an expression-istic project aimed at creating cathedral-like monuments atop each German town, with all the religious and mysti-cal underpinnings typical of that trend. These aspects of the

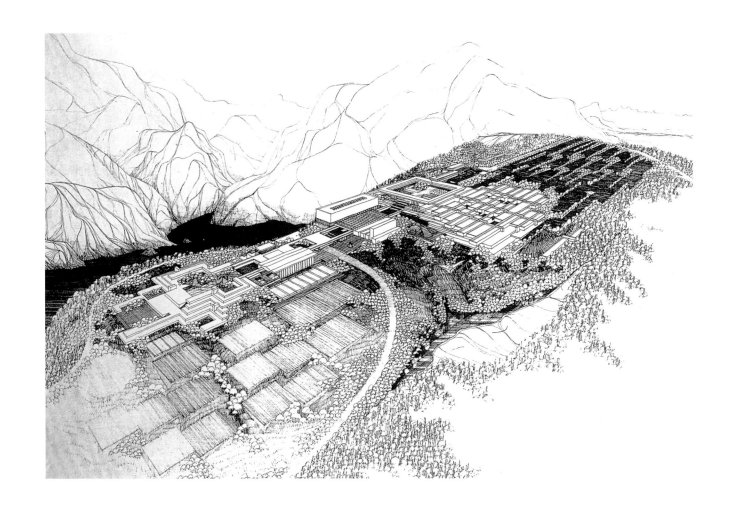

history of modernity had been somewhat forgotten and were being rediscovered at that time, notably through the "Visionary Architecture" exhibition at New York's Museum of Modern Art in 1960 and *The Architecture of Fantasy,* a volume that accompanied the show and was translated from the German and published in 1962.[13]

At SFU the "essence" of the design, in neoplatonic terms, is revealed not through a referential, planimetric diagram, but by its section. Viewed as an organic body, the university is unique in that it is composed of one single building whose very scale serves as a guarantor of the destruction of barriers between disciplines. The longitudinal section, however, reveals clearly the building's relationship to an architectural "type"—in Greek, *tupos* represents a print, imprint, mark or stamp. It is not the first time that the cross-section has been used in this way: Le Corbusier's 1936 design for the Ilôt insalubre no. 6 and his 1946 design for the unité d'habitation de Marseilles, or Alison and Peter Smithson's schemes for the Golden Lane housing project (1952–53)[14] are other prece-

below: John Andrews, Scarborough College, University of Toronto, Toronto (1965). Photo © Wayne Andrews/Esto

dents. Therefore, if the notion of type is given not as a shape or a planimetric historical reference to be copied (such as the Greek temple or the Roman basilica) but as an anatomical section through the different organs of a body, then, as Massey and Erickson write, the building "can grow from a relatively simple initial core, branch out and specialize as the opportunity arises,"[15] offering a robust spine of core functions on to which any predicted, or unpredicted, addition might be grafted as if on to a living body. Walking along the central path of SFU, then, is to experience a "peripatetic cognition"[16] that displays a "kinaesthetic perfume,"[17] in other words one becomes aware of one's own body movements while strolling throughout the building and experiences a physical, quasisensual pleasure. As such, what first appears to be a number of disparate elements actually becomes a united whole when you can walk through the main axis.

Looked at this way, SFU, which embodies the idea of a university campus building a new city from scratch, simply cannot be separated from the context in which it was born: the discussion that ended the Congrès Internationaux d'Architecture Moderne (in which many of those at McGill with whom Erickson was connected were active) and founded Team 10;[18] Max Bill's building for the Hochschule für Gestaltung, the school of design in Ulm (Germany, 1952);[19] Giancarlo De Carlo's Cappuccini University dormitories on the hills of Urbino (Italy, 1960; built 1962–64);[20] Eero Saarinen's IBM research labs in Yorktown Heights (NY, 1957–61).[21] This does not imply that the SFU project was influenced directly by these projects, only that it partakes of what Erickson called "synchronicity," the almost instinctive emergence in different cultural sensibilities of the same trend, and with each of these it shares something. With Max Bill's school, it shares the clarity of circulation; with De Carlo's dormitories, the hill siting and the Mediterranean reminiscences; with Saarinen's labs, the vast, quasi-monolithic dimension.

Furthermore, the question of the roof over the central mall at SFU, engineered by Jeffrey Lindsay, a follower of R. Buckminster Fuller, also brings up the question of advanced technological conceptions that were never far from Erickson's mind. (Lindsay's work appeared in *The Architecture of Fantasy* when it was published in New York.[22]) The glazed roof, spanning 91 by 41 metres (300 by 135 feet) and reinforced by girders fabricated from laminated, pressure-treated fir beams and high-tensile stainless-steel tie-rods, was an extraordinary engineering achievement. This technical feat belongs to a series of experiments that were seminal to spanning large spaces. In 1907, Alexander Graham Bell concerned himself with a space structure based on the tetrahedron, building a tetrahedral observation tower. From 1924 on, the German Hugo Junkers invented and produced three-dimensional geodesic structures.[23] In the late forties, Fuller was developing the geodesic dome (patented in 1954), based on the idea of a stressed skin stretched on three-way double-layer grid structures, which culminated in his inflatable dome for covering part of New York City in 1962.[24] Also in the 1940s, Konrad Wachsmann, the designer of Albert Einstein's house near Potsdam (1928), created an aircraft shelter 50 metres (164 feet) long for the Atlas Aircraft Corporation, before developing the standard joint for space frames built in lightweight aluminium. Wachsmann spread his ideas by teaching widely in schools in Europe and North America.[25] At the same time, Franco-Polish engineer Stéphane Du Chateau invented variations on the system for connecting three-way double-layer lattice space grids and Robert Le Ricolais helped Louis Kahn develop the high-tech "city tower" projected for his Philadelphia Civic Center (1956–57), the model of which was exhibited at the Museum of Modern Art in 1960.[26] Lastly, between 1954 and 1962, Skidmore, Owings and Merrill developed and built a two-way space frame of vertical intersecting trusses for Mitchell Hall, the Air Force Academy dining hall, at Colorado Springs.[27] This structure was raised into position using columns as jacks.[28]

The construction of SFU's mall roof draws on strong and well-established trends of technological research: the glazing is supported on a space frame of roof-trusses pre-stressed by horizontal spreaders, a principle Erickson would use again later on the glass roof crowning the Law Courts in Robson Square (1974–79). The roof at SFU can also be related to inquiry into crystallography, again recalling Bruno Taut's Gläserne Kette, the "Glass Chain," a group of artists and architects who advocated the construction of crystallized buildings, and it clearly alludes to a long series of experiments in glass structure.[29] During the 1950s and 1960s, a good example of architects' interest in transparency and its geometries is found in the work of Kahn's partner Anne Griswold Tyng, who, recalling the polyhedral solids in Plato's *Timeus*, attempted to reach the "geometric extensions of consciousness," a Jungian idea closely related to Erickson's notions of evanescence and infinity.[30]

Erickson was not directly involved in what could be called the McGill connections to these lines of inquiry, but the intense association of Canadian architects on major projects—especially the long-gestated Expo 67—led to constant exchanges. An important set of contacts was established by Moshe Safdie after taking his degree at McGill in

1961—his thesis being a proposal for dwelling cells suspended on a separate supporting structure—first with the firm of "Sandy" van Ginkel and Blanche Lemco, who had been active within Team 10 and who would lead the first stage of planning for Expo,[31] and then with Louis Kahn's office in Philadelphia, where the acquaintance with Anne Tyng was made.[32] As section head, architect and planner with Expo 67 between 1963 and 1964, Safdie would introduce many of the ideas derived from these contacts, including those in his experimental Habitat 67 in Montreal.[33]

Other aspects of these connections, all moving towards the megastructure in their search for systems that could accommodate large numbers of people, were occurring in Israel, where Safdie was born. Without a doubt, he knew about and circulated information on what was happening architecturally there, including Alfred Neumann and Zvi Hecker's Bat Yam Civic Centre (1958–63), the Faculty of Mechanical Engineering in Haifa (1960–64) and the apartment block of Ramat Gan in Tel Aviv (1960–65), all widely published at that time. This context—the van Ginkels' testing of new urban morphologies, Tyng's work on geometries of scale, Neumann and Hecker's polyhedral theory of crystals[34]—helps explain the rationale behind the shape of the reduced octagons covering the central space of Erickson's Man in the Community Pavilion at Expo 67, a project that was germinal to his thinking, and of the Man the Producer Pavilion of his close friend Guy Desbarats of Affleck, Desbarats, Dimakopoulos, Lebensold, and Sise.

Erickson in fact owes to conversations with Desbarats and Ray Affleck the next step in this synchronous inquiry, which was the concept, especially in using concrete, of "rawness" or brutalism—the aesthetic behind Affleck's Place Bonaventure, conceived almost exactly at the same time as Simon Fraser.

Brutalism also marks such well-published works as Paul Rudolph's Art and Architecture Building at Yale University (1958–64) and his Boston Government Service Center (1962–71); Kevin Roche's Ford Foundation (1963–68); Philip Johnson and Richard Foster's New York State Pavilion for the 1964 World's Fair, and John Andrews' Scarborough College (1965), about which Erickson wrote with admiration. Erickson distances himself from much of this work, but his sketch for the Graham House (1963) already reveals a brutalist influence, at least at the level of the rendering. Like many a late modernist, Erickson wanted architects to show the guts of a building and be honest, brutal, even ruthlessly rough, in their decoration.[35] The entire SFU is built of reinforced concrete with large spans and cantilevered floors. As Erickson wrote in 1966: "Because unfinished concrete cleaned by sandblasting or bushhammering is the basic structural and finishing material, it becomes as noble as any limestone."[36]

Brutalism is not a style but a complex body of ideas that suggests that architects have to unleash their imagination, avoid dampening creativity by an excess of knowledge, eschew anything that could hinder originality and inventiveness. It is an anti-theoretical theory, and it is strikingly sympathetic to Erickson's idea of locating right solutions through a test of instinct and imagination. One could find the same attitude, and the same adherence to concrete as its muse, in Dan Kiley, the great American landscape planner, or in Claude Parent and Paul Virilio, the French team that got its inspiration from the concrete bunkers of the Atlantic Wall.[37] Erickson clearly belongs with this tendency, and perhaps the best description of him is, as a magazine in 1990 called him, "le virtuose du béton" (the virtuoso of concrete).[38]

top: SOM (Skidmore, Owings
and Merrill), Mitchell Hall, US
Air Force Academy, Colorado
Springs, Colorado (1954–62).

bottom: Moshe Safdie,
Habitat 67, preliminary model,
view of the facades facing
the Saint Lawrence River,
Expo 67, Montreal.

118

Despite the anti-theoretical stance of a majority of architects in the 1960s, theory did strike back even at the most successful and talented. Theory caught up with the practice of instinct at the junction of two scales of action: buildings and cities, and so the fundamental theoretical question was formulated in the following way: "Can large buildings offer a substitute for the city?" This was the central idea of the discussions between Aldo van Eyck and the Smithsons, and it is still of interest today.[39] The illustrations Erickson chose to introduce in his essay on city-building, *Habitation: Space, Dilemma, and Design* (1966),[40] provide a clue to some of the difficulties he encountered. For instance, he inserted photos of the now-famous Dogon village in West Africa that had been so much at the focus of van Eyck's voyages and writings since his trip to the Dogon in 1960. In Erickson's booklet, one photo is wrongly captioned "Straw huts in Cameroon" and it is borrowed from Bernard Rudofsky's famous, but famously superficial, exhibition "Architecture without Architects" at the Museum of Modern Art (1964–65). The exhibition and the book, which met with instant and universal success, introduced the public "to a communal architecture, produced not by specialists but by the spontaneous and continuing activity of a whole people with a common heritage, acting with a community of experience."[41] Erickson found himself in a contradictory position. On the one hand, he argued that with society's accelerating scope of movement, technology and communications, the architect must think on a new scale that encompassed the whole city; on the other hand, the majority of the illustrations he inserted in the booklet alluded to a kind of pre-industrialized world architecture, vernacular buildings without signature, authorless monuments of various civilizations such as the Incas' Machu Picchu, the West Coast Haida

facing page, left: Paul Rudolph, Yale Art and Architecture Building, New Haven, Connecticut (1958–64). Photo © Ezra Stoller/Esto

facing page, right: George Candilis, Alexis Josic, Shadrach Woods, Berlin Free University, Berlin (1963–74), competition model.

villages, the Greek Islands' habitat, the urban setting of Marrakesh, igloos, tepees, earth constructs, the Japanese traditional *tokonoma*, or decorative alcove.

Erickson's understanding of vernacular buildings was global. His "dilemma" was that putting together the megastructure with the vernacular elements created a theoretical problem that was hard to resolve. Safdie had likewise attempted to resolve this difficulty by placing essential elements of the North African casbah or of the Pueblo villages on a huge structure, first with his McGill thesis project, then with Habitat 67, and obtaining what the French architects, members of Team 10 like Georges Candilis, would call "une casbah organisée,"[42] an organized casbah. Erickson, in the sleek, stepped, terraced waterfront project of Evergreen Building (Vancouver, 1978) and in the 60-acre Sawaber downtown housing development in Kuwait City (Kuwait, 1976), went on to attempt similar stacked and systematic urban villages of his own, while the Metabolist group in Japan (1960) or the American designer William Katavolos in *Organics* (1961) suggested it was perfectly possible[43] (to use Reyner Banham's terminology) to "clip-on" vernacular constructions to a megastructure.[44] There had been important propositions on these questions of reconciling feeling and scale since the mid 1950s, in such projects as Yona Friedman's "Spatial City" or Eckard Schulze-Fielitz's "Urban Systems,"[45] one aiming at creating an artificial topography by raising a super-grid, the other calling for a decentralized city able to integrate mobility. Archigram's "Instant City" (1968–69) unified fluxes and movements, situations and happenings, events and performances, embedding the global village into megastructures,[46] and Georges Candilis's Berlin Free University (1963), which was based on a gridiron, proposed a rigid diagram of orthogonal structures on top of random, diagonal cross-circulation.[47]

The influence of such proposals for an "artificial landscape" and for megastructures appears clearly in some of Erickson's projects, such as the Project '56 development for the West End of Vancouver, the amazingly multi-functional ensemble Cité des Terrasses in Montreal (1968) or the residential and commercial high-rise proposal at Fisherman's Quay in Vancouver (1969). However, the question still remains: Are "megastructures" to use Banham's term, or "space frames" as the giant mall at Simon Fraser University was referred to in 1966 when it was compared with the Vertical Assembly Building at Cape Kennedy in Florida[48] or "omnibuildings" as *Progressive Architecture* called them in 1968,[49] capable of creating a city? And, briefly stated, the answer still remains: probably not. The 1960s debate had already raised the issue about the relation between large buildings and the large city, notably in the discussion during Team 10's meeting of September 1962, when van Eyck stated the poetic thought that the house was a tiny

city and the city a huge house,[50] an analogical notion that both the Smithsons criticized.[51] Joseph Rykwert in his *Idea of a Town*, which first appeared in Aldo van Eyck's *Forum* (1963), affirmed that the city was not a natural or physical phenomenon but a human artefact,[52] while Christopher Alexander, an architect and a mathematician, argued against a naturalistic urban analogy. By this he meant that architects and planners should stop reducing the city's complexity to simplifying diagrams, such as the one suggested by the hierarchical tree structure that moves from the roots to the main trunk and the main branches, up to the twigs and out to the leaves.[53]

It was in this climate of debate about where a building ended and a city began, as ever-larger scales were envisaged for both, that, in 1967, Erickson/Massey was asked to offer a concept drawing for Lethbridge University in Alberta, and then, in 1968, for the master plan for the whole campus and for "Project One," a design for the first building, which opened for the academic year 1970–71. The same principles put into practice for SFU were applied at Lethbridge, that is, flexibility and openness, and a high degree of interaction between students and faculty. There was an important difference: whereas the SFU complex was open to the surrounding landscape and enclosed one of its own, for climatic reasons Lethbridge was made from one single, huge building.[54] After a few intermediary studies, Project One integrated academic and residential facilities in a building nine storeys high and 278 metres (912 feet) long, the rationale being that since learning and living are two essential aspects of education, they should take place under the same roof. Again the method practised for the SFU design was used, since the essence of the building was communicated through sectional drawings, with faculty offices and seminars on the 8th floor, labs on the 7th, a main concourse—similar to a ship's core deck—where everybody could meet outside the classrooms, and the library and residences on the lower floors. At each floor, a slanting outward of the building created an interesting articulation of the exterior facades. Again there was a significant dissimilarity: whereas at SFU it was the longitudinal section that clearly revealed the logic of the design, at Lethbridge it was the transverse section that ought to have carried out this function. However, there were revealed some of the shortcomings of the design since the section cuts through a host of opaque contrivances and contraptions, such as closed staircases, that clutter the space. Looking at Lethbridge, one is left wondering why the designer couldn't have opened up the whole interior towards the sky, creating a vast central mall surrounded by stepped, canted terraces or balconies criss-crossed by catwalks and capped by a pellucid, high-tech roof.

Today the massive building sits like a beached vessel run aground, on a coulee overlooking the valley of the Oldman River. Through its length and the flatness of its crowning, Lethbridge University engages in a poetic dialogue with the city's famous High Level Bridge (built circa 1890), which spans the nearby valley where the railway crosses.[55] The two strong horizontal lines create, visually at least, a vast artificial horizon that enhances the contours of the valley and the coulees, and, as Erickson writes, produces "a distillation of the elements into earth and sky."[56] Once more, the architect tries to supersede the traditional Anglo-American campus concept and attempts to transform it by building a single megastructure with its roots dug into the surrounding valley.[57]

Over and over again, Erickson refers to medieval universities, such as Oxford, the Sorbonne, Bologna or Al-Azhar in Cairo, which, precisely, were for him "educational marketplaces."[58] However, it must be noted that these ancient insti-

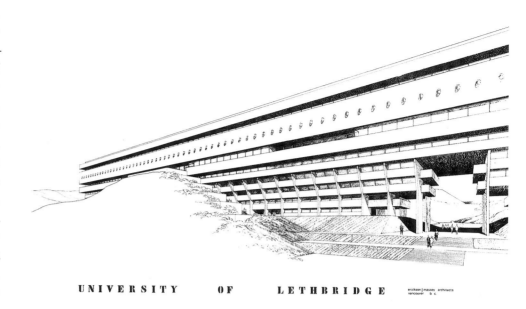

UNIVERSITY OF LETHBRIDGE erickson | massey architects vancouver b.c.

tutions were part of a city, and were rooted in their social, cultural and religious environments, and cannot be separated from their nurturing terrain and urban surroundings. It is true that both SFU's and Lethbridge's locations were not the choice of the architect, yet in both cases Erickson succeeded in using them to give form to a new institution, which is what architects should do. But is Lethbridge a megastructure? Strangely enough, while Banham published a description of the SFU campus in his 1976 volume on such megastructures,[59] he did not list Lethbridge, probably because, for him, it lacked some of the characteristics one would expect from such a spaceship: diagonal frames, additive and articulated structures, mechanical escalators, diagonal elevator ducts, Terrassenhäuser structures, multi-storey bridges and platforms, and so on. Actually, when one is confronted with the bulky and impressive profile of Lethbridge University, the images that primarily come to mind are either "surrealist" (such as Giorgio De Chirico's paintings) or nautical, or both. For instance, they recall the aircraft-carrier projects that Hans Hollein pasted together, in a dizzying and perverse way, in a series of drawings around 1964.[60] Erickson seems to have created—

Arthur Erickson with Geoffrey Massey, University of Lethbridge, Lethbridge, Alberta (1971), facade perspective study.

quality of a "megasculpture." To understand the fascination of this vast structure, one might recall two of De Chirico's "metaphysical" paintings entitled *Furniture in the Valley* (1927), which show dreamy and grotesque visions of furniture (bedsteads, armchairs, wardrobes and commodes) that have been moved outside and left in the open.[62] Like these images, looking at Lethbridge University from across the valley is like witnessing a huge commode that has landed there. Both in the actual landscape and in the painting, the juxtaposition of quotidian things against an empty background gives rise to the unsettling feeling that one is being confronted by something irrational and incongruous. Nordic expressionist painters, including Edvard Munch, called the anxiety that occurred in such infinite spaces Platzangst, and psychologists term it agoraphobia, the fear of open spaces.[63]

By playing on the scale of a wide, oversized edifice set "in the valley," then, Lethbridge University succeeds in uncovering some of the poetic, "metaphysical" potentials of the contemporary landscape. There are few places in the world where one feels more alone, more abandoned, more subdued by Earth's vastness, than in Lethbridge during the winter. However, allowing viewers to apprehend their solitude leads also to the recognition of the humbling, but significant fact that we live on a planet orbiting a star. Like a De Chirico painting, Erickson has succeeded in applying an artifice based on the principle of homesickness (*dépaysement* in French, *Heimweh* in German) that lets rise the uncanny feelings of dislocation and extraneousness that characterize many contemporary experiences. In a completely different way than Erickson does at sfu, at Lethbridge he manages to trick the senses with both brutal shifts of scale and complex manipulations of space, to trigger that bewildering sense of wonder for which his works are so well known.

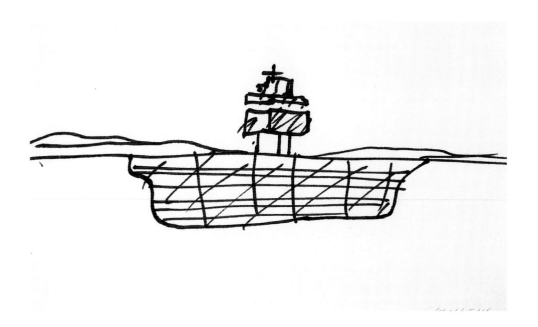

out of a mix of technology, the search for archetypal anatomies and the trust to instinct—a monolith, a huge uniform statue erected on the flat plains, and it stands like a megalith commemorating an ideal of sociability that the changing society around it made impossible to realize.[61]

Some argue that at Lethbridge Erickson did not succeed in creating a building of architectural significance that also redefined the traditional campus, that unlike Simon Fraser where he mediated historical archetypes with contemporary requirements, Lethbridge falls short of its goal to supersede the landscape and create a city of its own. Whatever the judgement on that issue, Lethbridge is undoubtedly a true work of art. If it isn't a megastructure, then certainly it has the

NOTES

1. Andrew Gruft, "Vancouver Architecture: The Last Fifteen Years" in *Vancouver: Art and Artists. 1931–1983*, Luke Rombout, ed. (Vancouver: The Vancouver Art Gallery, 1983), 318–31; and Ethel S. Goodstein, "Redeeming Modernism in the Context of Postmodernity: A Revisionist Analysis on the Architecture of Arthur Erickson" in *International Journal of Canadian Studies* 6 (Fall 1992): 25–43. These "critical" generalizations were known through Kenneth Frampton, "Prospects for a critical regionalism" in *Perspecta*, no. 20 (1983): 147–62.

2. Harold Kalman, *A Concise History of Canadian Architecture*, (Don Mills, ON: Oxford University Press, 2000), 574–75, and Carol Moore Ede, ed. *Canadian Architecture, 1960–70*, (Toronto: Burns and MacEachern Ltd., 1971), 246–53.

3. Arthur Erickson, *The Architecture of Arthur Erickson* (Vancouver and New York: Douglas & McIntyre and Harper & Row, 1988). See also Arthur Erickson, *The Architecture of Arthur Erickson* (Montreal: Tundra Books, 1975); Edith Iglauer, *Seven Stones: A Portrait of Arthur Erickson, Architect* (Madeira Park, BC and Seattle: Harbour Publishing and University of Washington Press, 1981); Barbara E. Shapiro and Rhodri W. Liscombe, *Arthur Erickson: selected projects 1971–1985* (catalogue) (New York: Centre for Inter-American Relations, 1985); *Arthur Erickson: AIA Gold Medal* (Washington, DC: AIA, 1986).

4. Arthur Erickson, "The Design of a House," *Canadian Art* 17, no. 6 (November 1960); reprinted in "The Artist's Eye. An Anthology of 40 Years of Essays on Canadian Art," *artscanada*, nos. 244/245/246/247 (March 1982): 98–100.

5. Geoffrey Massey, Arthur Erickson, "Museum Architecture 2: The Classical Solution," *Canadian Architect* 10, no. 8 (August 1965): n.p.

6. Abraham Rogatnick in *Architectural Review* 143, no. 854 (April 1968): 263–75. See also Giuseppe Mazzariol, "Il linguaggio di Erickson," *Lotus: An International Review of Contemporary Architecture*, no. 5, (Venezia: Bruno Alfieri Edizioni d'Arte, 1968), 161–87.

7. Arthur Erickson, *Memoirs, Cairo-Egypt, July 27th, 1950–Spain, March 1952*, unpublished manuscript, 31–32.

8. Arthur Erickson, "The Architectural Concept" in *Canadian Architect* 11, no. 2 (February 1966): 40. The whole issue is focussed on the Simon Fraser University buildings, 35–83.

9. Massey, Erickson.

10. Ron J. Thom, "Architecture of the Indefinite" in *Canadian Architect* 11, no. 2 (February 1966): 45–46, quote 45.

11. Paul Scheerbart and Bruno Taut, *Glass Architecture and Alpine Architecture*, Dennis Sharp, ed., (New York, Praeger, 1972).

12. Bruno Taut, *Die Stadtkrone*, (Jena: Diederichs, 1919); reprinted as *Die Stadtkrone*, mit Beiträgen von Paul Scheerbart, Erich Baron, Adolf Behne (Nendeln, Liechtenstein: Kraus, 1977).

13. "Visionary Architecture," exhibition (no catalogue) (New York: Museum of Modern Art, 1960); See also Ulrich Conrads and Hans G. Sperlich, *The Architecture of Fantasy: Utopian Building and Planning in Modern Times*, Christiane Crasemann Collins and Georges R. Collins, eds. (New York: Praeger, 1962).

14. Alison and Peter Smithson, *Urban Structuring, Studies of Alison and Peter Smithson* (London and New York: Studio Vista and Reinhold, 1967); Smithson, *Ordinariness and Light. Urban Theories, 1952–1960, and their Application in a Building Project, 1963–1970* (London: Faber and Faber, 1970); Smithson, *Without Rhetoric: An Architectural Aesthetic, 1955–1972*, Helena Webster, ed. (London: Academy Edition, 1997); Smithson, *The Charged Void: Architecture* (New York: The Monacelli Press, 2001); Dirk van den Heuvel and Max Risselada, *Alison and Peter Smithson: From the House of the Future to a House of Today* (Rotterdam: Uitgeverij 010, 2004).

15. Massey, Erickson.

16. Rogatnick, 264.

17. Lionel Tiger, "An Elaborate Hypothesis," *Canadian Architect* 11, no. 2 (February 1966): 42.

18. See Alison Smithson, ed., Team 10 Primer in *Architectural Design*, December 1962, 559–602; Alison Smithson, ed., *Team 10 Primer*, (London and Cambridge, MA: Studio Vista and MIT Press, 1968).

19. Karin Gimmi, ed., "Max Bill, architect," *2G, International Architecture Review*, no. 29–30, 2004.

facing page: Hans Hollein, *Aircraft Carrier City* (1963), felt pen on paper, 27.8 × 30.5 cm. Collection Musée National d'Art Moderne, Centre Georges Pompidou, Paris.

20. Vittorio Sereni et al., *Giancarlo De Carlo* (Milan: Bassoli Fotoincisioni, 1964).

21. Antonio Román, *Eero Saarinen: An Architecture of Simplicity* (New York: Architectural Press, 2003).

22. Conrads and Sperlich, *The Architecture of Fantasy*, ills. 118–19 and text 181.

23. Antoine Picon, ed., *L'art de l'ingénieur, constructeur, entrepreneur, inventeur* (Paris: Le Moniteur, 1997), 245.

24. Joachim Krauss and Claude Lichtenstein, eds., *Your Private Sky: R. Buckminster Fuller, The Art of Design Science* (Baden: CH, Lars Müller Publications, 1999).

25. Konrad Wachsmann, *The Turning Point of Building* (New York: Reinhold Publishing, 1961).

26. Louis Kahn, "Space, Order and Architecture," *Royal Architectural Institute of Canada Journal* 34 (October 1957): 357–77; Robert Le Ricolais, "Propos au sujet d'une architecture spatiale," in *L'Architecture d'Aujourd'hui*, no. 92, (1960), 192–93; Robert Le Ricolais, *Espace, mouvement, structure* (Nantes: Musée des Beaux-Arts, 1968); Peter McCleary, "Some structural principles exemplified in the work of Le Ricolais," *Zodiac*, no. 22 (1973): 57–69; Alison Sky and Michelle Stone, eds., "Le Ricolais, Robert" in *Unbuilt America* (New York: McGraw Hill, 1976), 165; David B. Brownlee and David G. De Long, eds., *Louis Kahn: In the Realm of Architecture* (New York: Rizzoli, 1991), 86 and ill. 80; Antoine Picon, ed., *L'art de l'ingénieur*, 153–54, 264.

27. Ernst Danz, *Architecture of Skidmore, Owings & Merrill, 1950–1962* (New York: Praeger, 1963).

28. John Borrego, *Space Grid Structures. Skeletal Framework and Stressed-Skin Systems* (Cambridge, MA: MIT Press, 1968).

29. Iain Boyd Whyte, ed. and trans., *The Crystal Chain Letters: Architectural Fantasies by Bruno Taut and His Circle* (Cambridge, MA: MIT Press, 1985); Regine Prange, *Das Kristalline als Kunstsymbol. Bruno Taut und Paul Klee: Zur Reflexion des Abstrakten in Kunst und Kunsttheorie der Moderne* (Hildesheim: Olms, 1991).

30. Anne Griswold Tyng, "Geometric Extensions of Consciousness," Graham Foundation for Advanced Study, n. d., published in *Zodiac*, no. 19 (July 1969): 130–62. See also Luca Rivalta, *Louis Kahn: La Construction poétique de l'espace* (Paris: Le Moniteur, 2003), 68–77.

31. Louis I. Kahn, "Design with the Automobile: The Animal World," interview with H.P. Daniel "Sandy" van Ginkel, *Canadian Art* 19 (1962): 50–55.

32. Louis I. Kahn, "Structure and Form," *Royal Architectural Institute of Canada Journal*, no. 11 (1965): 26–28, 32.

33. Moshe Safdie in *Beyond Habitat*, John Kettle, ed. (Cambridge, MA and Montreal: MIT Press and Tundra Books, 1970); Irena Zantovská Murray, ed., *Moshe Safdie: Buildings and Projects, 1967–1992* (Montreal: Canadian Architecture Collection, McGill-Queen's University Press, 1996); Wendy Kohn, ed., *Moshe Safdie* (London: Academy Editions, 1996), 40–42; Blake Gopnick, *Moshe Safdie: Habitat 67, Montreal* (Turin: Testo & Immagine, 1998).

34. Alfred Neumann, "Morphologic architecture" in *Royal Architectural Institute of Canada Journal* 40, no. 5 (May 1963): 40–47.

35. Reyner Banham, "The New Brutalism," *Architectural Review* 118 (December 1955): 354–61; reprint in Mary Banham et al., eds., *A Critic Writes: Essays by Reyner Banham* (Berkeley: University of California Press, 1996), 7–15; Jürgen Joedicke, "New Brutalism—Brutalismus in der Architektur" in *Bauen + Wohnen* 18, no. 11 (November 1964): 421–25; Reyner Banham, *Brutalismus in der Architektur: Ethik oder Ästhetik?* (Stuttgart: Krämer, 1966); Banham, *The New Brutalism* (New York, Reinhold Publishing, 1966).

36. Erickson in *Canadian Architect* 11, no. 2 (February 1966): 41.

37. Paul Virilio and Claude Parent, "*Architecture principe*": *1966 et 1996* (Besançon: Éditions de l'Imprimeur, 1996); reprint of *Architecture principe*, nos. 1 to 9; Paul Virilio, *Bunker archéologie* (Paris: Centre Georges Pompidou, C.C.I., 1975); reprint: (Paris: Éditions du Demi-cercle, 1992); Virilio, *Bunker Archeology: Texts and Photos* (New York: Princeton Architectural Press, 1994).

38. Jennifer Wells, "Le Virtuose du béton," *La Revue de L'impériale*, été (summer) 1990, 2–7.

39. Francis Strauven, *Aldo van Eyck: The Shape of Relativity* (Amsterdam: Architectura & Natura, 1998).

40. Arthur C. Erickson, *Habitation: Space, Dilemma, and Design* (Ottawa: Canadian Housing Design Council, 1966); in French: *L'Habitation:*

Espace, Dilemne et Solution (Ottawa: Conseil Canadien de l'Habitation, 1966), 8, ill. 7: "Huttes de paille au Cameroun" (sic!).

41. The exhibition was shown at the Museum of Modern Art in New York from November 9, 1964, to February 7, 1965. See Bernard Rudofsky, *Architecture without Architects: A Short Introduction to Non Pedigreed Architecture* (New York: Museum of Modern Art, 1965); reprint: Doubleday & Co, 1969, and Albuquerque, NM: University of New Mexico Press, 1987, paperback, 1998.

42. Aldo van Eyck's trip to the Dogon near Bandiagara started in mid February 1960. See A. van Eyck, "Architecture of Dogon" in *Architectural Forum*, September 1961, 116–21; van Eyck, *Forum*, July 1967, 30–50 (in Dutch); English version in *Via*, no. 1, 1968 (University of Pennsylvania); van Eyck, "A Miracle of Moderation" in *Meaning in Architecture*, Charles Jencks and George Baird, eds. (New York: George Brazilier, 1970), 172–213. See Francis Strauven, *Aldo van Eyck*, 380–91, 468.

43. William Katavolos, *Organics* (Hilversum: Steendrukkerij de Jong, 1961).

44. Reyner Banham, "Stocktaking," *Architectural Review* 127 (February 1960): 93–100; reprinted in Mary Banham et al., eds., *A Critic Writes: Essays by Reyner Banham*, 49–66: the term "clip-on" is used on page 57; see also Reyner Banham, "A Clip-on Architecture," *Design Quarterly*, no. 63 (1965): 3–30, reprinted in *Architectural Design* 35 (November 1965): 534–35; Banham, *Megastructure: Urban Futures of the Recent Past* (New York: Harper and Row, 1976).

45. Yona Friedman, "L'Architecture mobile" [1958, 1962] followed by "La théorie des systèmes compréhensibles" [1963], *Cahiers du Centre d'Etudes Architecturales*, no. 3–1, (Bruxelles: Paul Mignot, 1967); Rudolf Doernach, Hans J. Lenz, and Eckard Schulze-Fielitz, "Stadtbausystem," *Bauen + Wohnen* 21, no. 5 (May 1967): 176–78; Eckhard Schulze-Fielitz, *Stadtsysteme: Urban systems* (Stuttgart: Krämer, 1971–73); Yona Friedman, *Utopies réalisables* (Paris: L'Éclat, 2000).

46. Peter Cook et. al., eds., *Archigram* (London: Studio Vista, 1972); Dennis Crompton et al., eds., *A Guide to Archigram, 1961–74* (London: Academy Editions, 1994).

47. Georges Candilis, Alexis Josic, Shadrach Woods, *Building for People*, (New York: Frederick A. Praeger, 1968), 208–12 + the final plate.

48. "Space Frames," *Architectural Review* (April 1966): 245.

49. "Omnibuilding," *Progressive Architecture* 49, no. 7 (July 1968): 92–146.

50. Strauven, 397.

51. Ibid., 399.

52. Joseph Rykwert, "Idea of a Town," extract from "voor architectuur en darmee verbonden kunsten," *Forum*, no. 3, 1963; see also Rykwert, *The Idea of a Town: The Anthropology of Urban Form in Rome, Italy and the Ancient World*, (Princeton, NJ: Princeton University Press, 1976).

53. Christopher Alexander, "A City is not a Tree," *Architectural Forum* 122, no. 1, (April 1965): 58–62; no. 2 (May 1965): 58–61.

54. Trevor Boddy, "A Landscape of Ideas: Arthur Erickson Verbatim on the University of Lethbridge" in *Lethbridge Modern* (Lethbridge, AB: Southern Alberta Art Gallery, 2002), 42–53.

55. Antoine Picon, ed., *L'Art de l'ingénieur*, 118.

56. Arthur Erickson, "The University of Lethbridge: Project One," *Architectural Record* (May 1973): 115–23, quote 117.

57. Marco Sala, "Canada: Due Università; Universities Designed by Arthur Erickson," *Domus*, no. 75 (June 1975): 9–16, see 15 (in Italian and in English). See also Claude Franck, "Lethbridge: un paquebot dans la prairie," *L'Architecture d'Aujourd'hui*, no. 183 (January–February 1976): 46–50.

58. *Arthur Erickson: AIA Gold Medal*, 11.

59. Banham, *Megastructure*, 136.

60. Hans Hollein, *Aircraft-carrier City* (1964), drawing in Alain Guiheux, ed., *Collection d'Architecture du Centre Georges Pompidou* (Paris: Adagp, 1998), 159.

61. Paulette Singley, "Moving Solids," in *Monolithic Architecture*, Rodolfo Machado and Rodolphe el-Khoury, eds. (New York: Prestel, 1995), 24–35, with interesting considerations on the Greek *colossos*.

62. William Rubin et al., eds., *De Chirico* (Paris: Centre Georges Pompidou, 1983), ill. 83, 209, and ill. 85, 210.

63. William Rubin, "De Chirico et la modernité," in *De Chirico*, 9–37, esp. 10–11.

Affinity

"The Common Ground"

MOST OF US, when we first see Venice, are immediately enchanted by its luxurious silhouettes, colours, reflections and decorations. Erickson, in 1950, was captivated by its ground plan. He at once noted the modernity of its "ideal traffic system: the complete separation of pedestrian and mechanical modes of travel with no interruption or conflict between them."[2] He was fascinated by the difference between wide canals that move in a grand processional flow and narrow waterways that meander at a solitary pace, and by the different faces the pedestrian city showed as it changed level between "shallow or steep arched bridges,"[3] and its vistas fluctuated from the tunnel of an alley to the closed perspective of a square to the open panorama of the water.

In the same way, at Oxford, he had looked not at the buildings but at "the pattern of the town,"[4] at the colleges with their cloisters, gardens and courts screened behind a streetfront wall. It was not the face and features of individual buildings that caught his imagination but their patterns of approach and use, and especially the character of the space between them, like that in traditional Mediterranean villages, where communal space is created and defined by the dwellings that make its perimeter.[5] Such observations led to a determination to render urban architecture holistically. Indeed, all of Erickson's critical city works have been tied to this wider analysis: a deep reading of their current surroundings, the anticipation of what would likely grow up around them and a response that makes "a presence to clarify the whole."[6]

Erickson saw three basic elements at play in his work in city contexts: scale, level and line. Scale he regarded as a key device to anchor a new work to the urban fabric: occasionally, he adopted a scale and an approach to massing that typified the monumental city adjacent to them, but more often, he set up an opposing scale to emphasize a common pattern through counterpoint. By varying levels, he believed that the experience of the city could be enlivened and its inherent structure given a new, topographical meaning: to do this, he either cut through the existing plane (like a swath through an urban forest) or cut down into it (changing the level of the common grade) or floated structures above it. He saw line as fundamental to organizing vistas and to helping people moving through the city to read its geography. He inserted long low lines into the vertical city, drew imaginary lines in the air to "cast points of view and vistas out from them,"[7] or—as at the Canadian Chancery in Washington—"into enclosures of common ground."[8]

That "common ground"—the space between structures— became the fourth and most essential element among Erickson's urban affinities. He argued that walls should be regarded not so much as enclosing a building and establishing *its* shape as defining the shape of the empty space *around* it. In this

> "The city is a manmade landscape, representing in topography, form and even climate an ecological interdependence as delicate as nature. Every change in that stucture can be felt throughout it, like a tremor through a spider's web."[1]
>
> ARTHUR ERICKSON

Arthur Erickson, Project '56, sketch proposal for redevelopment of Vancouver's West End (1955).

communal space, Erickson saw civilization itself emerging in the relationship to common ground "which everyone possesses as an extension of himself."[9] Thus, Erickson's ideal city, like "the total building of the medieval city,"[10] is a great landscape of paths and steps, enclosures and openings, terraces, commons, glades, landmarks and walls. Its geographies are formed by a pattern of changing scales, levels, lines and vistas that are imperceptible without the crucial openings and interstices that carry one through.

Erickson's first exercise in city design was in 1956, for a vast site above English Bay in Vancouver's West End. Addressing how Vancouver might move from a small port city to the megalopolis its planners expected, Erickson looked upon the city, trapped between the ocean and the mountains, "as an island... whose growth was naturally upwards" and countered the inevitable array of apartment towers by proposing to cover the entire crown of the site's hill with two gigantic terraced towers.[11] These topographic forms swept back, floor by floor, to peaks of eighty and one hundred storeys, leaving a wide oval clearing as common space between them.

The project also generated a number of Erickson's persistent central ideas about the city. One is "cadence," staggering and terracing a building as it rises to give access to light, to set up vistas and to sculpt its face with light and shadow. Such cadences appear again and again, whether in abstract form at Expo 67, structuring Robson Square and its Law Courts inside and out, or setting off buildings from a ragged or colourless urban landscape as a set of hanging gardens, as on the surface of Vancouver's Evergreen building (1978) or visible through the colonnade of the Canadian Chancery (1983–88). Another is the idea of "a topographical profile," putting a skyline in dialogue with the natural landscape. For the West End, this was conceived as the vista of an undulating surface, spread over the city in consonance with its backdrop of mountains; at Robson Square it became an undulating mountain walk of its own, not a vista in itself but a set of viewpoints from which to gain them. These were steps towards a vision of "city-scale architectonics," in which individual buildings would be forgotten, while a vast, coherent cityscape would make "a city readable and life in that city memorable."[12] That remains the ideal to which Erickson's urban interventions aspire.

It is not surprising, then, that when Erickson was invited to revise the facade proposed for a new Vancouver headquarters for the forest products conglomerate MacMillan Bloedel, he instead proposed a study both of the site and of what an

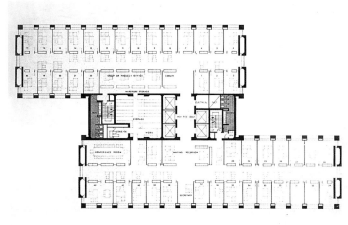

above left and below: Designed in 1965, the 27-storey MacMillan Bloedel building sits on West Georgia Street in downtown Vancouver. The photo collage from an early promotional brochure (below) shows the proposed tower dominating the skyline, while an early photograph of the completed work (left) shows a more nuanced relationship with its surrounding buildings. The tower, which included the headquarters of the namesake forest products company as well as rental offices, is built of site-cast concrete. Design team: James Strasman, Geoffrey Massey, Gary Hanson, Proctor Lemare. Photo © Ezra Stoller/Esto

above right: The plan comprised two towers slightly offset around a service core containing elevators, exit stairs, washrooms and maintenance rooms. The column-free space allowed for open-plan work areas (the secretaries' desks line the middle corridor of each tower) and private offices.

A dramatic contribution to Vancouver's skyline.

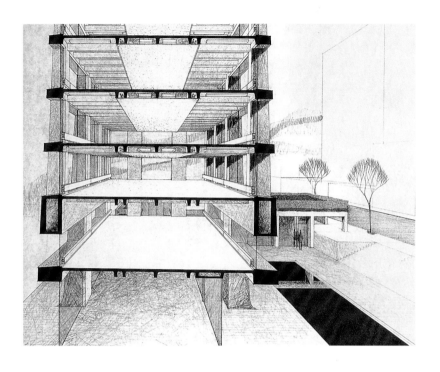

office tower might do to help clarify the city's downtown. The downtown core itself presented a chaotic picture in which visual density varied radically from block to block: glass curtain walls at one scale inserted themselves beside masonry facades at another, quiet space was absent and there was no differentiation between the character of movement or vista from one street or another. "The sense, the context to be given to the chaos of the contemporary city has not come through," Erickson wrote in 1964. "I don't think it will come through in the creation of Italian plazas, or the tidying up of an environment whose only excitement is its disorder… The forms of the city are waiting to be discovered and transformed."[13] What could a single building do to change this experience of the city and to help compose the one to come?

Erickson proposed two joined towers, set below the streetline and slightly apart, with a service core in the connection between them. By presenting only a narrow face to the descending line of the street at the side, he gained a quiet corner in which (working with John Landzius) to insert a grove of evergreens. This provided a natural landmark, reminiscent of the tree forms of the towers and of the purpose of its occupant. Erickson here adapted concrete into a monolithic structural language suggesting containment, geometry, repetition, strength, weight, mass, uniformity and solidity, all of which ran counter to the then scattered and varied pattern of the city. Setting the building back and down into a narrow water court, he reinforced the line of the roadway and sidewalk above it, but widened and dropped the vista from traffic on the street and gave different routes of different characters to pedestrians moving at different paces. As robust as possible, it engaged by sympathetic disengagement and by the tension in the slippage between its towers. "This," Erickson has said, "was my Doric building."[14]

In 1966, as the MacMillan Bloedel project was reaching completion, Erickson/Massey undertook a study of Vancouver's downtown peninsula to propose systems and policies that could bring architectural integrity to the growing city. They focussed the study on the vacant blocks to the south of the court house, proposing a gigantic government tower to straddle them. Around this would spread a layered system of transit, parking, shopping and services, linked by platforms from which blocks of differing heights would emerge. Although the plan only begins to suggest an original urban topography, it significantly advanced Erickson's investigation of the city, advocating different types of roadway and open space, each with a distinct character of its own. "The significant urban character of a city," he said later, "exists in… the streets, the squares, the vistas, the waterfront edges… how the city unfolds as you move through it."[15]

The downtown study led Erickson to increasingly radical ideas. He felt that a holistic architecture was inhibited by the enforced separation between buildings and that restrictions on sightlines and setbacks compartmentalized the street space into rigid geometries. Moreover, the tradition of zoning to reflect different uses seemed increasingly at odds with actual patterns of life. Erickson urged architects and urban planners to have the "courage to accept the raw face of truth," which was that "the ugly but vital aspects of the American city" came from its disorder.[16] Erickson was drawing on his knowledge of linguistics and on the communications theory of Marshall McLuhan to grasp this uncomfortable truth. He spoke of architecture as "a kind of language,… units of meaning which, put together, make sense out of… confusion," its buildings as phrases, city blocks as its sentences, sectors as

facing page, top left: Designs for the MacMillan Bloedel building emphasized the relationship the plaza creates between the street grid, the modified topography of the sunken plaza and the narrow, light-filled office floors. This sectional drawing also shows strategies for dealing with repetitive modules of space, a figure not often seen in Erickson's projects.

facing page, right and bottom: Erickson spent considerable design energy on the public faces of the building, an unusual interest for the firm but a matter of great concern to the client. These sketches show various possibilities for modelling the exterior surface. Because the exterior walls are structural, the designs show a classical approach to the rhythm of solids and voids. The final elevations used a module of 7-foot-square windows, without mullions, set deep in the concrete bearing walls. Further elevation drawings studied ways to heighten the rough simplicity of the towers' form and to dramatize their presence in Vancouver's business district.

paragraphs. But the necessary glue was its punctuation and syntax, which he saw in "the trafficways, the communication systems,… advertising… the… power pole and the street sign… the traffic interchange."[17]

Since his return from Japan in 1961, Erickson had seen the citizen of the communications age inhabiting not just a physical fabric but "an extended sense cage which gives him an awareness far beyond his physical limitations."[18] His next city works moved away from the solidity of the MacMillan Bloedel building to meet this. In 1969, he was awarded the commission to design, around the shell of a 1930s building in Ottawa, the new offices of the Bank of Canada and an adjacent set of public spaces. His first proposal was to enclose an interior courtyard with monumental concrete forms, pierced only by vertical slits that offered glimpses into a skylit garden. But then he transformed his design completely, rendering the blind walls in glass through which the inner garden court was visible and against which the solid city was reflected. He later employed the same strategy of presence through absence in proposals for the modern art museum in the Beaubourg quarter of Paris. The sides of the museum would disappear as they mirrored the streets around them, enclosing quite another city within.

The Beaubourg project was concerned with setting up the "most essential factor in the development of a culture—human interchange," both by reflecting the life of the space outside and by enfolding the common space within: "The traditional attitude is to think of the skin of the building as enclosing the building," Erickson wrote, but "the building skin can define the limits of the outside space and enclose it as effectively as the inside."[19] With the Osaka 70 pavilion, he shifts attention from the single building towards "comprehending the meaning of the whole." These exchanges between a building and its context were expressed by conceiving of a "structure responsive to everything around it," mutable and uncertain as the changing sky it captured.[20] But the passage through the mirrored leaning forms also works as a reflector of the temporary city built around it, suggests a Canada too vast to be painted in anything but light and evokes the infinite kaleidoscope of the sensory cosmopolis at large.

In 1972, the New Democratic Party of British Columbia won its first provincial election. The outgoing government had developed a plan for a fifty-five storey tower at the empty site of the three-block downtown core of Erickson's earlier study. The new government invited Erickson to rethink the project in terms of a wide-ranging downtown civic centre, with law courts, provincial government offices, public space and a cultural centre. In sympathy with the New Democratic ideal of social transparency and increasingly averse to the corporate tower, Erickson forsook the skyscraper and rigid hardscape of his previous plan. He laid a setback tower on its back, letting its recumbent form serve as the central feature in a "three-dimensional parkspine," "a landscaped pedestrian throughway" that broke the grid and plane of the city by cutting two rising and falling lines, one on the grid and the other against it, from one side of the peninsula to another.[21] Only the three blocks of the core went beyond the conception stage, but even at that scale Robson Square is an astounding experiment in urban form.

At the south end, under a great slope of glass, the pedestrian passage moves through the Law Courts in "a street arcade in which the action of justice would be seen."[22] As the structure descends to the north, the walkway moves over a hardscape of waterfall and pool, and close to a ground level of connecting courts. Under all of this is the administrative machinery of government. At the northern end, the plaza spreads beneath Robson Street—the dip making the existing street the visual focus of the whole scheme—and mounts towards the neo-classical building of the old court house. The symbolism is elaborate: justice visible as the basis of civil society; government discreetly unassertive and at the level of the everyday to administer that society; the arts rising, dependent upon civil order but wholly independent of its mechanisms; the moving citizenry as the focus of all of them.

As prospects of carrying the walkway underground in a second layer dwindled, the geometry of the project was deliberately variegated and softened. Powerful elements did remain: the glass roof of the courts; the repetition of concrete "knees that bow to the people"[23] and carry the indoors out; the delicate meeting between the great knees and the huge metal truss of the roof; the repeated forms of the paving and planters. By the last phase of the project, converting the old court house to a civic art gallery, Erickson's team was referring to the mixing of a "classical language" with the "kinetic planes" of his own concrete grammar,[24] and his critics to a "fuzzing of design philosophies" in place of "tough and hardened certainties."[25] But Erickson would argue that, in the context of the times, he chose to move away from the rigorous order of the "total building"[26] towards a renewed preoccupation with ensemble, that acropolis of elements where casual and even discordant juxtapositions are allowed.

When, in 1977, he was invited to design another Vancouver super-block to house offices for the Government of Canada, Erickson again resisted both tower and streetfront, hiding the ceremonial presence of government within two gigantic space frame tubes that shelter a public garden. These great airships drew on the space frame of the Law Courts to

top: Arthur Erickson and Geoffrey Massey, Centre du Plateau Beaubourg, Paris, competition model (1971).

bottom: Arthur Erickson with Geoffrey Massey, Canadian Pavilion, Expo 70, Osaka.

right: The Robson Square site in downtown Vancouver, first known as the Three Block Project, included the original courthouse and two empty blocks to the south that belonged to the provincial government. Erickson's team studied the urban surroundings with landscape architect Cornelia Hahn Oberlander, whose association with Erickson began at this time, and concluded that the three blocks could be developed as a low-level, low-density landscape with considerable planting, rather than as a (politically unpopular) tower.

facing page, top left: Erickson's proposal centred on a public rooftop garden above the government office spaces in the central block, organized around a reflecting pool and three-level waterfall. The concept separated pedestrian and public transport (buses) from car traffic. Oberlander used hanging roses, bamboo and native Pacific Northwest clinging plants.

facing page, top right: The main gallery of the new Law Courts features concrete "knee frames" supporting a large sloping space-truss topped by a tinted glass roof. Inside, terraced galleries contain courtrooms and judges' chambers.

facing page, bottom: Together, the three blocks of Robson Square (the Vancouver Art Gallery [1983] on left, provincial government offices [1978] at centre and Law Courts [1979] on right) form an urban meadow, a figure derived from Erickson's visits to China (extensive street planting) and iconic city green spaces (Central Park in Manhattan), updated through innovations both visible (the system of ramps and stairs in the central block) and invisible (the incorporation of the water from the reflecting pools into the fire-safety system). Robson Square creatively encourages pedestrians to use the building through an extensive system of landscaping, ramps and stairs, parks, retail space and a sunken plaza. Design coordinators: Bing Thom, James Wright, Rainer Fassler.

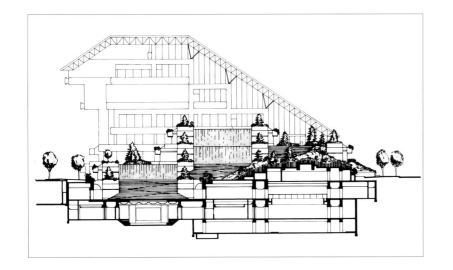

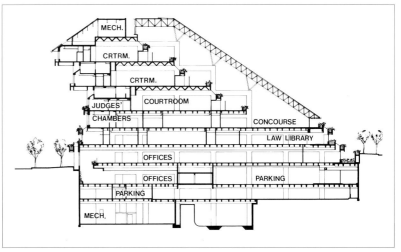

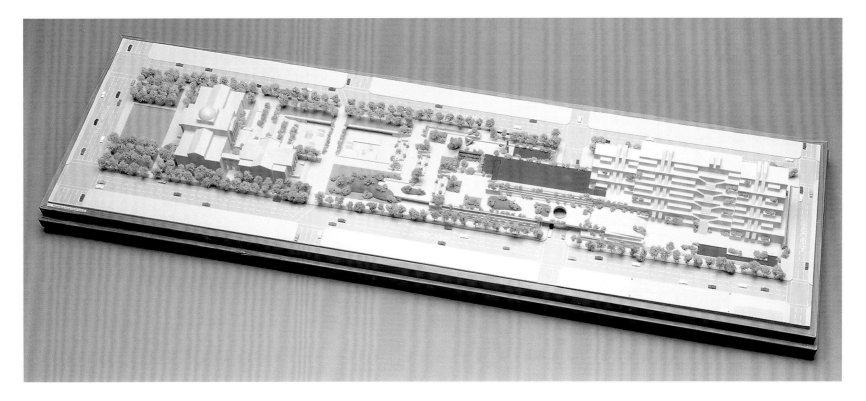

above: Arthur Erickson, Proposal
for Government of Canada
Building, Vancouver, presentation model (1977).

right: Arthur Erickson, presentation model for Roy Thomson Hall,
Toronto (1976–82).

establish glass in configurations that would make them, from outside, both transparent and reflective. This strategy accommodated the uncertainty of the city at its developing perimeters by shaping it for probable vistas from buildings that would be built above, across and below.

Such was also the argument of Roy Thomson Hall in Toronto, begun in 1976. The idea was to mediate, with glass rising above concrete ground planes, between the masonry and brick of the old downtown edge and the glass blocks of a new business quarter. Toronto is a city of walls, and Erickson's luminous draped canopy of glass was to counter it with shimmer and a sense of celebration. Costs modified the shape and sheen of the pavilion, but inside, Erickson developed his argument about public space: it has an "absolute restraint and honesty of structure,"[27] which Francisco Kripacz emphasized with a precisely calibrated flat palette of pearl grey which, with the cluster of hanging tubes beneath it, seemed both to reveal and dissolve the heavy roof. Prevented by traffic constraints from opening the hall to the thoroughfare, Erickson chose to deny it a grand entrance altogether, floating the plaza straight off the street and setting up entry to the hall as a long streetline marquee. This focusses all promenade and ceremony inside the great glass tent.

Roy Thomson Hall was a project in a city overwhelmed by streets and walls, and peculiarly resistant to joy or glamour. Los Angeles presented the same challenge in reverse: a city without walls and whose streets seemed to be disappearing, but with a penchant for colour and display. In July 1980, Erickson won the competition with developer Cadillac Fairview for a massive downtown mixed-use project that would form a link between the city's performance centre and its commercial heart. His proposal for three connected towers was, as Rem Koolhaas suggested, "a single gesture . . . a compo-

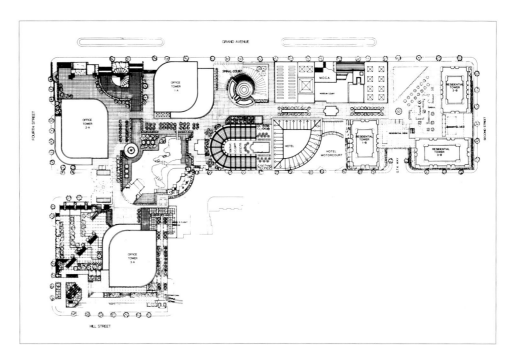

sition of towers, connected by a lower . . . linear element, . . . a kind of maelstrom, through which a variety of culture disappears underground," but which was united by repetition and by reference to "a metaphysical order."[28] Given Erickson's distaste for the tower, he might have developed the whole site as a continuous horizontal form; instead, he distributed elements of different scale and height—an Erickson acropolis—and then united them as the varied faces of a trenched promenade—an Erickson street. But the extension east to the Music Center was dropped, the design of the residential and hotel blocks was parcelled out, the streetscaping was forgotten and the south tower, key to the "stratification" of the scheme, was never built. The strength of the project, which lay in the coherence of street, bridge, plaza and tower, was therefore denied. Much of the kinetic vitality also was lost as, one by one, the cultural and artistic interventions were dropped. But, as Koolhaas recognized, building on this neutral site was like designing for a void, and Erickson's deep readings of context had perhaps too little to draw upon to make the ensemble persuasive and impregnable.[29]

Arthur Erickson with Gruen Associates and Kamnitzer & Cotton, master plan for California Plaza, Los Angeles (1980–ongoing).

Arthur Erickson, Fresno City Hall,
Fresno, California (1987–90).
Photo © Mark Darley/Esto

By 1984, when the Canadian Chancery design for Washington, DC, was being prepared, Erickson was willing to address this problem of the vacant site or setting by beginning to argue that the solution was to make the surroundings appear as if they were made for the building, rather than the reverse, so that it orchestrated its own skyline and its own approaches. These terms fit the situation in this imperial stretch of Washington, with its stringent and stylistically exact planning rules. The most obvious solution was to build a box with a large interior court, but Erickson wanted a truly public building that communicated an open welcome without surrendering its necessary grandeur. Hence he faced the project east, away from the ceremonial avenue and towards a popular pocket park and walkway. He set most of the small

chancery block to the west and opened the space between them to a court of water, hanging gardens and concrete. At the core of the court, the Native artist Bill Reid's sculpture transposes Emanuel Gottlieb Leutze's 1851 painting *Washington Crossing the Delaware* into an anti-heroic, Canadian view of the inevitability of dissension and dissent. The same subtle ironies inform Erickson's treatment of the literal classical elements he was compelled to use: he confines them to open colonnade and portico, and then carefully omits lintels, cornices and capitals, hollowing out the columns to show how little they have to do with substance or structure. Above, the chancery staggers back in tiers of horizontal garden terraces that rise to its most powerful feature, a great Erickson view line on its top floor, structuring a panorama of the capital city, as if in a vista from the north. Meanwhile the earth and its resources in that north are celebrated as white marble moves to dark vegetation, metal and water; government is set in an open stoa, the ceremonial stair doubles as a public walkway, and the quiet court, like the mosque of Cordoba, made ready to accept every visitor as its proprietor.

Soon after the opening of the Chancery in 1989, Erickson's practice began to implode, and it was not until 1996 that he could begin work (in partnership with Nick Milkovich) on another significant city building, the Museum of Glass in Tacoma. But his California office had, in its last years, designed two major city works that were realized alongside

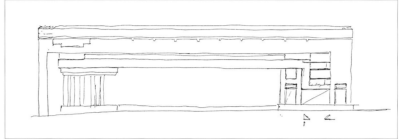

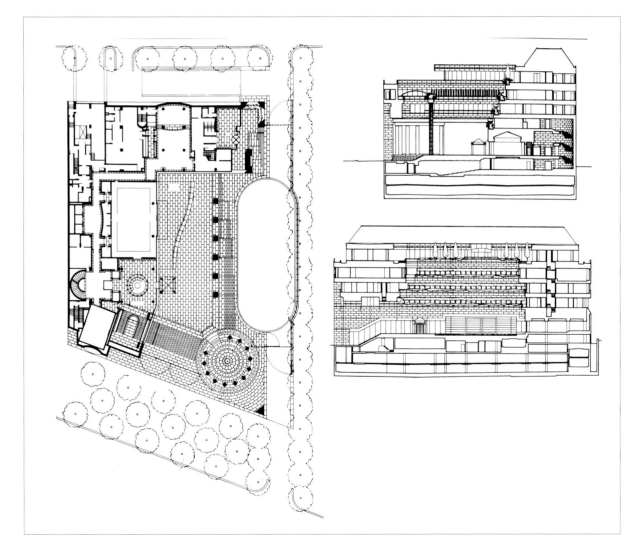

top left: Erickson undertook the preliminary design of the Canadian Chancery in Washington, DC, amid widely publicized controversy. The government under Prime Minister Pierre Trudeau awarded Erickson the commission over the four finalists from a field of seventy-one firms recommended by the selection committee.

top right: Unpolished Adair marble cladding, a vehicle entrance for dignitaries, a colonnade (a Washington planning requirement), as well as cornices and a base line all suggest classical Mediterranean models, such as the textual descriptions of Pliny's villa at Laurentium.

left: The terraced office levels culminate in an open roof surrounding the ambassador's office. A rotunda whose twelve columns represent Canada's ten provinces and (then) two territories, and a pool with Bill Reid's bronze sculpture *The Spirit of Haida Gwaii* liven the courtyard. The plan shows the negotiation between the diagonal of Pennsylvania Avenue and the open space of John Marshall Park.

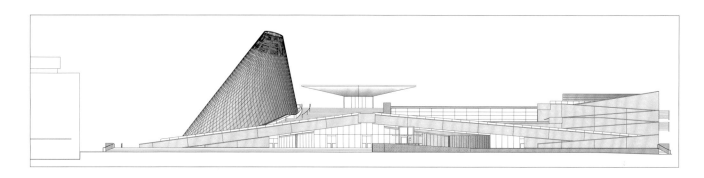

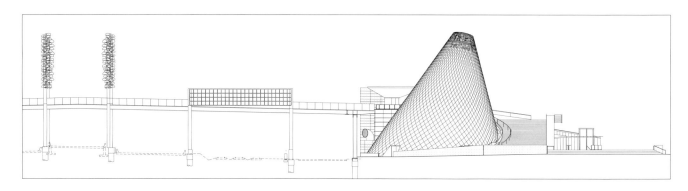

top: The 81,000-square-foot Museum of Glass (2002) sits in a waterside museum precinct in the downtown harbour of Tacoma, Washington. As in many projects, Erickson counts on the similarities between glass and water: reflectivity, clarity, fluidity. The two materials are both juxtaposed and made equivalent, for example, in the use of pools to reflect and animate the concrete surfaces and to symbolize the harbour. The rooftop plaza is a public space, open twenty-four hours a day, with access to the Thea Foss Waterway. Design team: Nick Milkovich, Wyn Bielaska, Anne Gingras, David Liang, Randy Bens, Gerald Penry.

centre: The 88-foot cone, which houses the Hot Shop amphitheatre, recalls the sawdust burner towers once familiar in the Northwest and gives the museum an iconic compositional centerpiece. Stairs wrap around the cone's exterior, joining the entrance lobby and the upper concrete terraces.

bottom: The building is dominated by a tilted, steel-covered cone that contains ovens for glassmaking demonstrations. Visitors enter from a glass bridge that extends from the nearby Washington State History Museum over the highway.

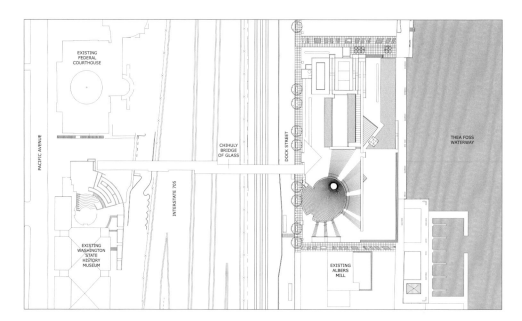

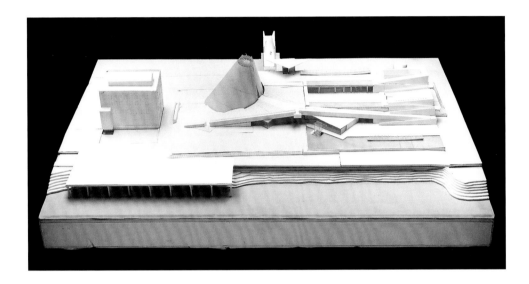

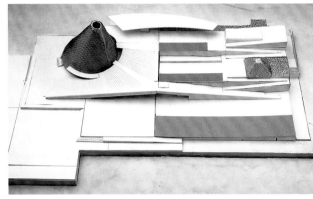

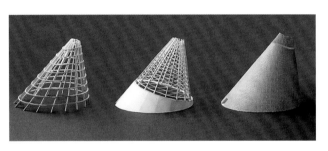

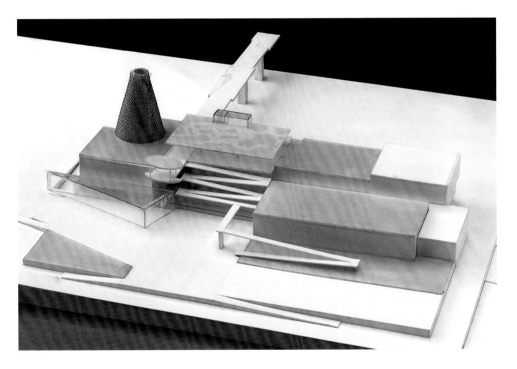

These study models show Erickson searching for a topography in which to situate the museum. They manipulate sectional and volumetric relationships to create the image of a citadel, hilltop village or acropolis, rather than a single building. The volumes and shapes echo both the distant mountains and industrial landscape of the harbour.

143

the Chancery: a convention centre in San Diego and a new city hall in Fresno. Both use dramatic changes of level to turn the flattest urban wasteland and buildings that traditionally set up monumental barriers into penetrable structures of rising and falling public open space. San Diego, set on a strip of ex-wharfside beside a transport corridor, reminisces on the derricks of the old port, which governed its structural system, and its round glazed corridors speak within to the memory of crystal palaces and without to the railway termini of the nineteenth century. The scale of the Tacoma museum is quite different, but its situation is identical, and the strategies that Erickson employed were similar. But where Fresno draws on Erickson's Hamma project in Algiers to establish a monumental geometry, and where San Diego articulates its system through complex repetitions, Tacoma is a complicated topographic ensemble of almost random forms that renders itself into an utterly generous and simple urban park.

Six ideas inform the design of the Museum of Glass. First is the orchestration of the surroundings—harbour, freeway and warehouses—into a "concrete landscape."[30] Second is the creation of a structure of crossing and intersecting planes, like a path up a mountainside or a cross-section through its geological structure. Third is the tension produced by the cantilever, most evident in the roof hovering over a glass entry pavilion. Fourth is an homage, in the shape of the furnace tower, or "hot shop," and in the wide plaza that sets it apart, to Le Corbusier's Chandigarh. Fifth, advancing the discussion of elements he had introduced at the core of the Chancery and then developed as the governing motif of a 1990 beach house in California,[31] is a symbolic program that brings the four elements into play with one another, reminding us that glass itself is earth made molten by air and fire, and cooled into fixed forms by

water. Last, and in the same elemental vein, is the introduction of a sort of fundamental topography. No vegetation is used: the garden is a geometry of ground, sky, water and light. The light is anchored by the view of Mount Rainier, a pyramid of snow in the natural landscape that resonates with the dominating feature of the concrete landscape, the hot house—not simply in its shape but also in its ever-changing luminosity.

At Tacoma, Erickson developed and fused many strategies for making a distinctive space and a characteristic presence within a changing urban assembly. He transposed his experiments in stacking a single material into a ziggurat, as at the Sikh temple (Vancouver) and the Expo 67 pavilion, to a different scale and plane in order to achieve a counterpoint to the linear urban melody. As at San Diego, the conversion of roof into plaza made a park from dead space, and as at Robson Square, diagonal cuts into the hardscape changed the pace and perspective by forcing a physical experience of shifts in level. As at Evergreen, he made a hillside of concrete rise where the grid falls apart at the water's edge, and as at Roy Thomson Hall, he set a light-catching, free-form object into an opaque plaza, using light as well as plasticity to isolate a sculptural landmark amid the brick and masonry walls of the streetscape.

Erickson thus eloquently reasserts his central ideas about the patterns of the city: that civic space is about giving an aesthetic structure to movement, that civic buildings find their affinity with their surroundings not by deference but by setting up an answering presence that brings the whole into clearer focus, and that in the city "there is no such thing as a freestanding structure. It cannot exist without the specificities of its site."[32]

NOTES

1. Arthur Erickson, in discussion with the author, 1999–2004.
2. Arthur Erickson, unpublished draft of memoirs. Used by permission of the author.
3. Ibid.
4. Ibid.
5. Arthur Erickson, *Habitation: Space, Dilemma, and Design*, pamphlet published by Canadian Housing Design Council, Ottawa, 1966, with an appendix, 1967, 13.
6. Erickson, in discussion with the author.
7. Ibid.
8. Ibid.
9. Ibid. See also Erickson, *Habitation*, 37.
10. Erickson, *Habitation*, 31.
11. Trevor Boddy, "Erickson's Vancouver: Cityscape 1," *Vancouver Sun*, June 12, 2004.
12. Erickson, *Habitation*, 22, 27.
13. Arthur Erickson, "The Weight of Heaven," *Canadian Architect* 9 (1964), 48.
14. Erickson, in discussion with the author.
15. Arthur Erickson, "Revitalizing Our Cities," *Plan Canada* (Nov/Dec 1993), 48. See also Erickson/Massey, "Proposal for Block 61 and the Downtown Core, Vancouver," *Architecture Canada* 43, no. 8 (August 1966), 42.
16. Erickson, "The Weight of Heaven," 48.
17. Ibid.
18. Ibid.
19. Erickson, *Habitation*, 36–37.
20. Arthur Erickson, *The Architecture of Arthur Erickson* (Vancouver/Toronto: Douglas & McIntyre, 1988), 76–77.
21. Arthur Erickson, *Block 51-61-71: Three-Block Concept*, mimeograph submission in the office papers of Cornelia Hahn Oberlander, partial copy at Canadian Centre for Architecture, Montreal, 27. Also Erickson, in discussion with the author. See also Bing Thom, Erickson's project director on Robson Square, in discussion with the author, and Arthur Erickson, unpublished draft of memoirs. Used by permission of the author.
22. Erickson, in discussion with the author. See also Erickson, *Block 51-61-71*, 36.
23. Erickson, in discussion with the author.
24. Barbara Shapiro, "The Three-Block Project: Classism [sic] and Modernism Combined," *West Coast Review* 15, no. 4 (Spring 1981), 10.
25. Trevor Boddy, "Arthur Erickson's Vancouver Art Gallery," *Section 'a,'* (April 1984), 5–6.
26. Erickson, in discussion with the author.
27. Ibid.
28. Rem Koolhaas, "Two Competition Projects for Bunker Hill in Downtown Los Angeles," *Trace* 1, no. 3 (July–September 1981), 10.
29. Ibid., 15.
30. Erickson, in discussion with the author.
31. Elizabeth McMillan, "Balboa Residence" in *Beach Houses: From Malibu to Laguna* (New York: Rizzoli, 1994), 162–67.
32. Ibid.

The MacMillan Bloedel Building, Vancouver

THIS REDOUBTABLE office building sits like a pair of giant interlaced trees in Vancouver's downtown, its tapering forms somehow managing to represent and evoke MacMillan Bloedel's involvement in the rude and wild forestry industry. The sunken entrance courtyard adds to the sense of an urban forest setting, creating a topographical site for the towers.

This symbolism helps to explain why MacMillan Bloedel is *sui generis*. Shaped by a sculptural hand for pointed local purposes, it tilts against the standard-driven development of the conventional office tower. Nevertheless, as a tower, it is a visible landmark in the city and, therefore, has an identifiable composed facade. The search for an interweaving of inside and outside, landscape and building, is limited to the lower floors; the upper floors are determined by the requirements of rentable office space on the inside and are reined in by the need to proportion wall and window on the outside.

The MacMillan Bloedel building makes clear that Erickson's architecture, though not often driven by a priori theories or ideologies, is antipathetic to that emblem of modern architecture, the elevator. For Erickson's cosmology, the elevator is anathema, momentarily disconnecting visitors from the experience of the building, removing crucial markers of distance, structural systems and materials.

Detail photographs show how the poured-in-place concrete walls are optically and physically coarse, recalling rough-hewn logs. At another level, the concrete-bearing wall facades speak eloquently of a mythical symbiosis between architecture and gravity. The seven-foot sheets of glass buried deep in the concrete walls seem, despite their regularity and proportion, private and protective, indicating domestic life rather than corporate power.

More remote views uncover some of the irregularities of the building, irregularities that at their best humanize or naturalize the urban concrete office building, but at the risk of also isolating it. This strategy makes it a solitary building that stands apart from its surroundings to engage them from a lonely distance.

Ricardo L. Castro & David Theodore

147

Robson Square, Vancouver

ROBSON SQUARE is a familiar place. Like Simon Fraser University, it is a favoured setting for the numerous movies and television series filmed in Hollywood North. While the square's famous "stramps" turned out to be something of a non-starter, aggravating pedestrians, roller bladers and skateboarders alike, the idiosyncrasies of the streetscape attract lunchtime sun seekers, twenty-first century *flâneurs* and tourists.

The photographs capture a striking mix of neo-hi-tech Law Courts and urban garden. In images and experience, the apt renovation of a historic building into a municipal art gallery overcomes the artificiality of the place—or rather its artificiality makes it attractive. This is no place, yet it holds its own as a destination in a city of natural park settings: English Bay, Stanley Park, Point Grey.

The camera uncovers a panorama of artificial nature—shrubbery, trees, water, waterfalls—that strains to reinterpret the urban plaza as urban park. The Law Courts, with its long concrete beams and greenish expanse of sloping glass, rises not so much as an urban cornerstone but rather as the machine in the garden.

Once more, here is a building that explores a post-and-beam structural system. And once again *entasis* is conspicuous by its absence. The vertical columns and the horizontal beams, as in the Helmut Eppich house, have the same dimensions.

The photos show a haunted space where the old modernist idea of transparency = democracy collides with the problem of transparency = surveillance. The photos here also function as a cinematic montage, or more accurately a storyboard, evoking a story by the juxtaposition of spaces, actors, tectonic elements and topography.

Ricardo L. Castro & David Theodore

158

The Canadian Chancery, Washington, DC

LIKE THOSE of a classical monument, the qualities of the Canadian Chancery in Washington, DC, are visible up close. Detail photographs show the unusual care taken with joints between stones, proportions of elements and the contrasts of materials: brass and limestone, aluminum and water.

Even a casual encounter—visitors often approach the chancery when en route to nearby Washington landmarks—shows a building both at home with its confining site, willing to stand out from its bland neighbours but also deferential to the many significant buildings nearby. The success of this strategy of simultaneous autonomy and interdependence is different for each condition. As an object on its own, the building revealed in the photographs is a sumptuous, carefully modulated historical postmodernism. But as an attempt to mediate with, say, I.M. Pei's addition to the National Gallery, or the far away Capitol building, the architectural gestures are as flat as they are for other recent Washington architecture: too controlled by design guidelines and formal references, unanimated by the staid program.

The same artificiality confuses any attempt to see the chancery as a building in the United States that represents and evokes Canada and Canadians. The rhetoric of ornament is part of the historical blip of postmodernism. The basic symbolism of the columns in the corner rotunda—one for each province and territory—seems forced. Additions like the Bill Reid bronze sculpture, a spirit canoe filled with legendary Haida characters, will delight visitors, because they seem more harmonious as works of art than the building.

As in Erickson's houses, it is as a spatial composition, part intellectual, part experiential, that the chancery is most persuasive. Consider the subtle choreography of stairs, porticos, doors and car ramps, where architecture is understood as manipulating changes of level and establishing a new topography. Most visitors will approach the chancery on foot: the monumental stair is for them. But they quickly see that the ceremonial access is for cars bringing diplomats and dignitaries securely to and from rendezvous with the ambassador and his entourage. Visitors are welcomed; dignitaries are honoured. Thus, the approaches build in a decorous hierarchy of spaces

Ricardo L. Castro & David Theodore

161

The Museum of Glass, Tacoma

Arthur Erickson conceived the Museum of Glass in Tacoma, Washington, as a true urban fragment rather than as a simple architectural object. Working in collaboration with Nick Milkovich Architects and in close consultation with project designer Wyn Bielaska, he designed the building to stimulate the sustainable development of Thea Foss Waterway, once a barren and polluted area of the city's waterfront.

The museum and parking facilities lie under a series of terraces and stairs, which enhance movement around the building and into the surrounding neighbourhood. For example, from the museum's rooftop terrace where visitors arrive, a "bridge of glass" links the museum with the city's downtown art district and the waterfront esplanade below.

Giving focus to this open urban plaza is a monumental leaning cone, sheathed in diamond-shaped stainless shingles, which houses a hot-shop amphitheatre with several glass studios and galleries. It looms over the site, a powerful emblem that evokes regional themes: the shape of Mount Rainier clearly visible in the distance or the long-gone, cone-shaped, wood-burning structures of the Pacific Northwest.

The skillful articulation of planar architectural elements—terraces, stairs, ramps and reflecting pools, each enhanced by the use of an earth-coloured concrete—as well as the links the complex makes to its surrounding landscape, are, in their stillness, alluring themes for the camera. However, this urban fragment seems to beg for moving images that can capture the continuous shifting of shape, light and colour in this invented mineral topography.

Ricardo L. Castro & David Theodore

The Man Who Wasn't There

To SEARCH for a defining essence of Arthur Erickson's architecture is to confront a paradox. Since his projects include single- and multiple-family dwellings, corporate headquarters, commercial office buildings, two university campuses, exposition pavilions, a museum, an embassy and numerous urban planning schemes, he cannot easily be classified as a designer of a particular building type without doing injustice to the sheer variety of his work. In an age of increasing professional specialization when architects have become as typecast as Hollywood actors, Erickson has remained a generalist, a trait that links him to other twentieth-century modernists such as Mies van der Rohe, Frank Lloyd Wright and Louis Kahn. Stylistically, his work proves no easier to categorize, and at various times has been labelled critical regionalism, megastructuralism, brutalism, third- or fourth-generation modernism. Although such tags sometimes helpfully identify significant features of his architecture, none can encompass its total range, as a consequence of which they all are incomplete and more often than not misleading.

Revered in Canada while scandalously underappreciated elsewhere, a situation that speaks volumes about our current celebrity-obsessed culture, Erickson is the antithesis of the architectural star, the media personality whose biography is the fodder for gossipy journalism. This is not to claim that he has not enjoyed his fair share of publicity, simply that he has never cultivated a signature design style, the *sine qua non* of global professional recognition and the transformation of architecture into a brand identity. On the contrary, it is almost as if the profusion of stylistic idioms in his work was intended to throw critics off the track, although I would defy anyone to identify an architect less concerned with currying favour among tastemakers and more frequently oblivious to their views than Erickson.

Known for building in concrete, he also has worked extensively with wood, glass and steel. Renowned for his sensitivity to the climate and landscape of British Columbia, he also has built in the snowy plains of Alberta, the arid deserts of Saudi Arabia and the temperate meadows of England. Erickson has worked variously as a solo practitioner, a principal in several partnerships and a collaborator on projects whose large scale necessitated the co-operation of many offices. The creator of iconic buildings such as Simon Fraser University and the University of British Columbia Museum of Anthropology, he has designed many other projects every bit as singular but far less well known. His work is simultaneously regional, national and international, a product of a system of core values realized in vastly different modes of architectural practice.

Yet despite this heterogeneous profile, the unity, coherence and focus of Erickson's architecture are beyond doubt. His work is grounded in a cogent world view that has been remarkably consistent over the course of his career. Erickson has written not merely on his own work (to which he remains an indispensable guide) and on the situation of architecture and urbanism more generally but also on politics, law, society, education and culture. If he has a public persona, it must surely be as the conscience of Canadian architecture, the stern and frequently chastising voice that for more than four decades has decried mediocrity and challenged architects, politicians, business leaders and ordinary citizens to settle for nothing less than the best buildings and cities of which their society is capable. Erickson's Scandinavian roots propose him as the Kierkegaard of his profession, a figure whose scathing criticism of the architectural status quo rarely has boosted his popularity but inevitably has introduced key questions and raised the level of public debate. As he notes:

> I am concerned with what our civilization is all about, and in expressing this in buildings. Everything I do, everything I see is through architecture. It has given me a vehicle for looking at the world. I am not involved in the aesthetics of architecture or interested in design as such. I'm interested in what buildings can do beyond what they look like, and how they can affect whole areas and people's lives. I have never done a building where I didn't at least attempt to see it in a new philosophical or social way. I could have asked questions in any field, but I am doing it through my buildings.[1]

If Erickson is both an architect and a philosopher of civilization, this latter dimension of his work, a complete assessment of which must await the publication of his collected essays and criticism, also illuminates his own national identity. Like Northrop Frye and Marshall McLuhan, two thinkers who exemplify the Canadian tradition of cosmopolitan and socially engaged cultural inquiry at its liveliest, he too began

"to think globally and act locally" long before this credo became a slogan on bumper stickers during the 1980s. Consider in this regard the astonishingly prescient discussion of cultural globalization developed in his essay "Sharing—The Choice Is Ours":

> It is first of all essential to appreciate the import of context as it pertains to human cultures. For a long time it was believed that we were moving towards one world—that modern transportation and communication would soon homogenize indigenous cultures into a single world mix. But in fact an opposite trend has set in and everywhere minorities are moving toward emancipation and self determination... Everywhere this new regionalism asserts itself and the one world concept promoted by the technological super-powers no longer has the attraction it once seemed to have... We are learning to respect the fact that a solution for one time and place is not the solution for another.[2]

Sensitive to the unique geopolitical situation of Canada, which is intimately tied to the United States, the British Commonwealth and Europe, yet mindful of its own special path, Erickson has long possessed a knack for deftly balancing the regional, the national and the international. Rejecting the universalism of McLuhan and its underlying catholic faith in a future global community linked by technology, Erickson has been skeptical of cultural homogenization in all its forms, especially in its American variety. Although he has worked in the United States and built there, not always successfully in my view, the overall arc of his career delimits a sustained critique of postwar American modern architecture, the degraded legacy of the International Style whose

172

generic glass towers and expressionless industrial parks today ring most large North American cities.

Nowhere is this critique more evident than in Erickson's blistering attacks on the disasters produced by importing American architecture and urban planning into developing countries such as Bali and Afghanistan. As he noted in his 1978 address to the Congress of the International Union of Architects in Mexico City, " In America, a new kind of anonymous city was born—Anywhere, U.S.A.—to spread everywhere in the late sixties and seventies as unchallengeable American expertise became in universal demand, giving birth to Anywhere, The World."³

Approaching architecture as a social technology capable of transforming the world (for good or ill), a stance that distinguishes him from the many architects who have shed the idealism of the 1960s, Erickson refuses simplistic dichotomies that supplant critical thought. His ideas resist encapsulation in sound bites and remind us that rational public discussion of urban and architectural design once was possible—and may well be possible again in the future. Interrogating our relationship to the contemporary technological environment, he rejects sharp distinctions between the aesthetic, the ethical and the political, a predilection that lends his thought a European quality and distances it from the empirical and pragmatic orientation of much North American thinking. Erickson's sensitivity to the prospects and dangers of life in industrial society, one shared by McLuhan and Frye, may well be where his national identity is at its strongest. Although he has called Canada "a country without a culture,"⁴ I believe that he in fact exemplifies an indigenous tradition of Canadian technological criticism whose proponents sought to articulate their own sense of intellectual responsibility as

Canadians while simultaneously engaging with the broader world. This legacy has been well summarized by philosopher Arthur Kroker:

> What makes the discourse on technology such a central aspect of the Canadian imagination is that this discourse is situated *midway* between the future of the New World and the past of European culture, between the rapid unfolding of the "technological imperative" in American empire and the classical origins of the technological dynamo in European history. The Canadian discourse is neither the American nor the European way, but an oppositional culture trapped midway between economy and history. This is to say that the Canadian mind is that of the *in-between*: a restless oscillation between the pragmatic will to live at all costs of the Americans and a searing lament for that which has been suppressed by the modern technical order.
>
> What is at stake in the Canadian discourse on technology is always the same: the urgent sense that the full significance of technological society… cannot be understood within its own narrow terms of reference. For Canadian thinkers, technological society jeopardizes at a fundamental level the received traditions of western culture, and makes of our fate as North Americans a journey, almost a skywalk, into an unknown future.⁵

More so than most Canadian architects, Erickson has occupied this domain of the *midway* and the *in-between*, surveyed its terrain and accepted its challenges as his own. Seeking a "third way" that might transcend oppositions between the global and the local, international modernism and local vernaculars, collectivity and individuality, the new world and the old, building and landscape, technology and craft, utopian optimism and wistful nostalgia, he has pushed these distinctions beyond their commonplace meanings and in so doing greatly expanded our sense of what is possible in architecture. Central to this radically syncretic enterprise is Erickson's belief in the primacy of relationship, a provocative challenge to traditional definitions of architecture as built form. As he observes:

> I suppose it is human nature to abhor perpetual change and to seek permanence in seemingly stable monuments. No doubt we search for finalities and conclusions in order to allay the uncomfortable flow of life. Though we like to think in terms of solutions to explain phenomena and to answer problems, it is evident that there is nothing as final as a "solution," nor even a final answer to a question, for any answer must give rise to further questions. Nor can we put as much faith in the forms representing "solutions" as we have in the past. For these forms are now recognized as having established only a brief though cogent relationship with their environment. Seen as the frozen embodiments of relationship, such forms have temporary value, enabling us to turn our attention to the more serious matter of better perceiving these relationships. Just as science has found that the essence of matter is energy, so the architect must understand that the essence of form is relationship, and that is all that really matters.[6]

In this affirmation of temporality and flux as the limiting conditions of both architecture and human existence, Erickson seems to approach the perspective of an Asian philosophy such as Buddhism with its understanding of life as change. One cannot help but be struck by the distance between this axiom and the underlying conceit of most architects to design for the ages and realize buildings whose immortal-

ity is beyond doubt. Although the many years Erickson spent in Japan and his deep knowledge of its culture have clearly marked his architecture, a point to which I shall return, I want to suggest that this influence is more philosophical than stylistic and resides most deeply in his exemplary sensitivity to relationship as the primary architectural category. If forced to devise a label for Erickson, I would call him a critical relationist for whom form, style, function and context are necessary yet insufficient determinants, elements in a complex equation that the architect uniquely solves in each building.

Two design strategies present themselves throughout Erickson's work and suggest the means by which he has been able to realize an architecture of relationships. The first I call the inverted totem pole. Its primary characteristic is an endlessly varied suspension and interruption of monumentality, a deployment of form whose symbolic resonances are deliberately truncated so as to create an architectural "in-between" whose monumental impulses are visible, yet held in check. Consider one of his lesser known projects, the 1957 Grauer garden terrace and cabana, whose eight tulip-shaped shells for the roof sprout from hollow steel pillars in a riot of festive exuberance. Reaching for the sky, the Moorish forms of the roof and the vaults created beneath them evoke the royal prerogatives of an invisible potentate. Rendered in fibreglass, the lightness of this material, evident in its colour and texture, undercuts any potential bombast and instead lends the canopy the lightness of a sheet billowing in the wind. Erickson would have frequent recourse to this strategy of selecting materials whose formal or structural role in a design produces a sense of counterpoint, using wood or concrete in a manner that surprises or even startles.

One of the most prominent features in his architecture is its employment of mass, especially vertical forms, in a manner whose self-confidence and insistent materiality evoke the totem poles of the Kwakwa̱ka'wakw (Kwakiutl) Native people he long has admired. Like the totem pole, Erickson's architecture typically lacks ornament and generates meaning by the carving away and reduction of form. Its surface might be bare concrete or wood but always proves visually arresting. This process is evident in the MacMillan Bloedel office tower, whose punched-out windows instill the concrete mass of the building with an improbable lightness. Where many architects would have created a ponderous monolith, Erickson realizes a balance between strength and openness. The MacMillan Bloedel building also conveys a majestic impulse, for, like the totem pole, it is a family crest of sorts, a declaration of heraldry asserted not by a Native clan but by a prominent business family of the Pacific Northwest.[7] The symbolic resonances of the corporate skyscraper as a visible representation of economic might have been widely noted, yet Erickson's brilliant conceit is to in effect rewrite the history of this building type by deploying its earliest structural form, the solid load-bearing wall, in a manner that demonumentalizes it, inverting while not altogether cancelling its totemic value.

Not surprisingly, it is in the University of British Columbia Museum of Anthropology that the inverted totem pole strategy becomes most prominent in Erickson's work. No one who has visited the museum or viewed photographs of it can doubt the dramatic grandeur that radiates from its post-and-beam construction and location atop a cliff overlooking the city of Vancouver's harbour. Like the MacMillan Bloedel building, the manner in which the museum springs forth from its rootedness in the earth is wondrously sublime.

Writing in his 1947 essay "The Ideographic Picture," painter Barnett Newman conveys the junction of aboriginal and modernist form in a manner that seems equally applicable to Erickson's architecture:

> The Kwakiutl artist painting on a hide did not concern himself with the inconsequentials that made up the opulent social rivalries of the Northwest Coast Indian scene; nor did he, in the name of a higher purity, renounce the living world for the meaningless materialism of design. The abstract shape he used, his entire plastic language, was directed by a ritualistic will toward metaphysical understanding. The everyday realities he left to the toymakers; the pleasant play of nonobjective pattern, to the women basket weavers. To him a shape was a living thing, a vehicle for an abstract thought-complex, a carrier of the awesome feelings he felt before the terror of the unknowable. The abstract shape was, therefore, real rather than a formal "abstraction" of a visual fact, with its overtone of an already-known nature. Nor was it a purist illusion with its overload of pseudoscientific truths.[8]

Just as Newman derived inspiration from Native forms, so I would argue, did Erickson, finding in the abstract shapes of their paintings and vertical totem poles a bold intimation of the metaphysical. Like so many artists of the twentieth century, he is a keen admirer and a knowledgeable collector of aboriginal art, discerning in it the living forms identified by Newman as the vehicle for the abstracted forms of his architecture. The chimneys of the Eppich house or the University of Lethbridge, which counteract the predominantly horizontal layout of these buildings, exemplify this vocabulary of

abstract monumentality. At once connecting these structures to the surrounding landscape, these functional vertical forms also convey a powerful yearning. Yet nothing would seem more false than to construe them as mystical or otherworldly, for Erickson's architecture is resolutely material and intimately grounded in the texture, colour and reflectivity of its building components. Its rootedness in the earth neither promises nor delivers transcendence but reveals the pleasures of incarnate form that pull one closer to a place rather than beyond it.

Nowhere is this more evident than in the precast concrete columns and channelled beams of the Great Hall of the Museum of Anthropology, whose resonance with the Native objects on display exemplifies the congruence between vertical form and metaphysical gesture. For like the Northwest Coast Native peoples, his forms are typically non-anthropomorphic and rarely, if ever, evoke the human body. The Native paintings are, like the art produced by Newman and countless other postwar modernists, often non-representational, reminders of Erickson's notable indifference toward the Vitruvian paradigm of Western classical antiquity that enshrined man as the basis of architectural proportion in forms such as the column, what he refers to as "the vitality and strong presence that belong to the human figure, with which we are preoccupied."[9] In realizing buildings that are people-friendly in their built form yet anti-humanist in their philosophical underpinnings, Erickson encourages us to acknowledge that humanity is not "the centre and reason for existence," as "today we are being chastened by a growing awareness of our more humble role in the scheme of things."[10] Valuing an architecture that is responsible to nature, the environment and its own formal integrity in ways that frequently eclipse its role in glorifying human beings, he has pursued a more reflective path than many of his colleagues. Expressed differently, one might claim that Erickson has consistently emphasized these other dimensions of buildings so as to complicate our relationship to the world. The turn towards context and relationship in his architecture is but a longer and more rewarding journey to self-knowledge and ultimately a more robust appreciation of the human condition.

Where Erickson's architecture differs from much postwar modernism (think, for example, of Jackson Pollock and the tradition of abstract expressionism) is in its complete absence of anxiety, let alone any hint about the psychology of the architect. Claustrophobia and its opposite, agoraphobia, are nowhere to be experienced in his buildings. Entering them is to enjoy a sense of expanded possibilities, a freedom of spatial movement that invites exploration. And in the realm of detailing, the meetings of corners, the finishing of surfaces and the introduction of hardware and service systems, Erickson's architecture conspicuously avoids overdesigned fussiness, the nervous tics that often compensate for a weak design. His buildings neither fetishize technology nor shy away from it when necessary for the realization of a specific end. Similarly, the private side of domesticity is treated with admirable directness and empathy in his Eppich and Bagley Wright houses, in stark contrast to the generally minuscule and dark bedrooms that play second fiddle to opulent living rooms in the work of modernists such as Richard Neutra and John Lautner.

Nor does the integration of Erickson's buildings with their settings generate any discord, for few living architects have more perfectly inserted their work into diverse environments. As he notes, "Too often we think that the site exists merely to enhance a building, but we can learn from the ancient Greeks or any of the villages of the Mediterranean that a site can be made more beautiful by the buildings placed on it."[11] In the mouths of most architects, such words would sound hollow and self-serving, yet one need only visit the Eppich house (built on the site of a dump) or the Museum of Anthropology (built adjacent to concrete gun emplacements later incorporated into its design) to realize that Erickson makes good on this claim by truly enhancing these sites through his architecture.

His relationship to modernism is suggestively illuminated by reference to the work of Vancouver artist Gordon Smith, his earliest client, and like Erickson a stylistic polymath whose heterogeneous work defies classification. In his painting of a key landmark of the city, *Burrard Bridge,* completed in 1953, the same year that Erickson designed the painter's first house, Smith reveals a sensibility that parallels that of his friend and collaborator. The bridge is inseparable from its setting, wedged into the dense materiality of the city in a manner that evokes the later insertion of Erickson's second Smith house into its forest clearing, or the University of Lethbridge into the Alberta prairie. Both artist and architect favour bold horizontal and vertical lines that compose a geometry of lattice grids that remains asymmetrical. Abstract, yet deeply marked by colour and texture, Smith's painting, like Erickson's architecture, takes its inspiration from a specific site. Urban subject matter engaged many artists during the 1950s, yet it is telling that, like Smith, Erickson treats the city not as a source of anxiety but as a palette of spatial forms grounded in the reality of daily experience and radiating dynamic energies.

facing page: Kwakwaka'wakw house posts at Gwa'yasdam's, 1955.

Working throughout the 1960s and 1970s when many North American cities experienced political and social strife as urban planners watched helplessly on the sidelines, often while cities were quite literally burning, Erickson never ceased to believe in the metropolis. His urban schemes refuse to conceive architecture apart from the fabric of the metropolis and represent the last effective employment of modernist city planning on a large scale. In the rare instance, such as California Plaza, where Erickson was forced to modify his initially ambitious master plan at the request of developers, the result was a predictably disappointing separation of its office

towers and cultural facilities from the life of the street. Viewing his strongest legacy of this period, Vancouver's Robson Square, from a contemporary standpoint, it appears a precious bridge between a veritable dark age of the metropolitan imagination still traumatized by the failures of urban renewal and our own contemporary moment in which the city is once more back on the agenda in the work of quite different practitioners such as Rem Koolhaas and Diller Scofidio + Renfro. As with all of Erickson's work, Robson Square is also the expression of a philosophical credo, the critique of Western individualism, that the architect formulated with characteristic probity:

> Fifty years hence it may seem almost inconceivable to us what we meant by "individualism." Yet its alternative— organic collectivism—is by no means a new phenomenon belonging to the future. In the early middle ages of our own civilization each man saw himself as part of a pattern—a divinely sanctioned one—and he acted and behaved according to his role in that pattern. He saw his physical surroundings only as manifestations of that pattern and built his cities to express it in a single continuum of buildings culminating in the fantastically embellished cathedral. This continuity, this sense of pattern, role and purpose, is just beginning to make sense to us now that our persistent pursuit of individual destiny—exemplified in cities where each building proclaims itself in defiance of its neighbors—begins to be seriously questioned.[12]

Robson Square is perhaps the most literal inverted totem pole in Erickson's architecture, a skyscraper laid out and stacked horizontally, rather than vertically. Transparency in the administration of justice forms one key determinant of the complex, and the interrelation of commonly separated spaces and programs (law courts, parks, commercial development, an art museum) the other. "When I came to the realization that the law is simply another aspect of our culture, with no independent existence or inflated status… I concluded that justice had to be seen to be appreciated. Our law courts should be less a house of ominous retribution than a civics lesson in community standards. So aside from a layout for normal security precautions, we decided our mandate would be to open the courthouse to the public and to the street."[13] Indeed, the degree of public access to the law courts remains startling by contemporary American standards. Visiting them in late 2004, I entered the glass atrium through the rooftop garden entrance and saw judges, lawyers and clients circulating in its open expanse. Police officers, armed guards or closed-circuit television cameras were nowhere to be seen, and access to the courtrooms was uncontrolled and fully public, hardly the situation found in an American courthouse these days, when metal-detector security and identification checkpoints have become common.

As the most complex manifestation of Erickson's ideas about relationship in architecture, Robson Square suggests his engagement with Japanese architectural aesthetics. Circulation through the complex is not channelled or defined; the visitor can begin or end at any point. As Erickson observes:

> The orient has a different view of space. The pattern of space does not follow the human path because there it is symbolic. In the Japanese house, space wells out on all sides like a series of concentric circles until it merges with the space of nature, symbolized by the garden. Around the core of the house is wrapped the divisible living space, and

Gordon Smith, *Burrard Bridge* (1953), oil on canvas, 59.7 × 85.1 cm, Collection of Mr. Bruce Williams, Ottawa, Ontario.

> around this an inner veranda and then an outer veranda, with the border of the garden carefully laid out; and then the garden itself, expanding beyond its boundaries into untamed nature. In this non-directional order, the path and the different uses of space for sleeping, eating or visiting can be anywhere; spaces are arranged like a series of folding screens to be put up or down at will.[14]

Defined by the architect as "merely a container for a classic, bushy Olmsted park,"[15] Robson Square is truly constructed around its greenery rather than vice versa. Its landscaping is more than a mere exterior to the building and functions as what the Japanese call *engawa*, the grey space or intervening area between inside and outside.[16] Erickson's architecture abounds with this type of spatial play that frustrates clear distinctions between interior and exterior, often by the introduction of labyrinthine forms such as gardens or foyers that deflect and deter one from a set itinerary. Walking through the rooftop park landscaped by his long-time collaborator Cornelia Hahn Oberlander, I found the experience of its multiple viewing levels and shifting perspectives more akin to peeling an onion than moving in a straight line towards a destination. Indeed, the interior design of the courts and offices appropriates this sensibility wherever possible, employs open space and movable partitions in lieu of the endless corridors and rigid spatial divisions found in many government buildings.

In the several mirrored buildings and pavilions that Erickson has designed, one finds other affinities between his architecture and Japanese culture, what the architect calls "the idea of infinity... The aspect of ambiguity—the uncertainty of what is substance and what is space... the impermanence and mutability of life."[17] His 1970 entry to the competition for the Centre du Plateau Beaubourg reflects the surrounding Marais neighbourhood in its facades, reduplicating its visual form while adding landscaped amphitheatre terraces which compose a multi-level labyrinth. A year earlier he had employed

a similar idea in his Canadian pavilion at the 1970 Expo in Osaka. Its surfaces sheathed in mirrors produced a vertiginous play of reflections that pushed the ambiguity between interior and exterior space to the limit. While mirrors concentrate and focus identity, they also have the potential to derealize it, and it is in this latter direction that Erickson's mirrored buildings, including his design for the Bank of Canada, travel. The stable unities of culture, the nation and the economy are momentarily interrupted in these designs, in which relationships are multiplied to the point of infinity.

Erickson frequently has observed that architecture contains but a limited number of themes that reappear in a few archetypes, yet "human mutability is such that the archetype can be approached but never obtained."[18] Here, the architect reveals his affinities with Northrop Frye and other intellectual voices of the 1960s and 1970s who embraced structuralist explanations of human culture as systemic and rule-governed. If the greatest paradox of Erickson's architecture is its attainment of a high degree of individuality through the replacement of individualism by relationship, one can only admire the gracefulness with which the architect simultaneously occupies the interior and exterior of his oeuvre, realizing in and through his buildings the ultimate disappearing act.

NOTES

1. Edith Iglauer, *Seven Stones: A Portrait of Arthur Erickson, Architect,* Madeira Park, B.C.: Harbour Publishing and Seattle: University of Washington Press, 1981, 19.

2. Arthur Erickson, "Sharing—The Choice Is Ours" (address to the American Society of Planning Officials, Vancouver, B.C., April 14, 1975), 1–2.

3. Iglauer, 25–26.

4. Iglauer, 20.

5. Arthur Kroker, *Technology and the Canadian Mind: Innis/McLuhan/ Grant* (Montreal: New World Perspectives, 1984), 7, 12.

6. Arthur Erickson, *The Architecture of Arthur Erickson* (Montreal: Tundra Books, 1975), 207.

7. On the totem pole, see Audrey Hawthorn, *Art of the Kwakiutl Indians and Other Northwest Coast Tribes* (Vancouver: University of British Columbia Press and Seattle: University of Washington Press, 1967), 343.

8. Barnett Newman, "The Ideographic Picture," in *Barnett Newman: Selected Writings and Interviews,* ed. by John P. O'Neill (Berkeley: University of California Press, 1992), 107–8.

9. Iglauer, 61.

10. Erickson, *The Architecture of Arthur Erickson* (1975), 53.

11. Ibid., 23.

12. Erickson, "Sharing—The Choice Is Ours," 5.

13. Arthur Erickson, *The Architecture of Arthur Erickson* (Vancouver: Douglas & McIntyre, 1988), 118.

14. Ibid., 43.

15. Ibid., 118.

16. On this concept, see Kisho Kurokawa, *Rediscovering Japanese Space* (New York: John Weatherhill, 1988), 54.

17. Erickson, *The Architecture of Arthur Erickson* (1988), 77.

18. Ibid., 131.

Bibliography

WRITINGS BY ARTHUR ERICKSON

"Design of a House: Robert M. Filberg House, Vancouver." *Canadian Art,* vol. 17, no. 11 (November 1960): 338–42.

"The Weight of Heaven." *Canadian Architect,* vol. 9, no. 3 (March 1964): 48–531.

with Geoffrey Massey. "Museum Architecture: The Classical Solution." *Canadian Architect,* vol. 10, no. 9 (September 1965): 58.

"Habitation, Space, Dilemma and Design." Lecture at the Vancouver Art Gallery, Vancouver, November 22, 1965. This is the third in a series of public lectures sponsored by the Canadian Housing Design Council, Ottawa. In the collection of the Canadian Centre for Architecture, Montreal.

"The Architectural Concept: Simon Fraser University." *Canadian Architect,* vol. 11, no. 2 (February 1966): 60–62.

with Geoffrey Massey. " Proposal for Block 61 and the Downtown Core, Vancouver." *Architecture Canada,* vol. 43, no. 8 (August 1966): 42–43.

"The Architecture of Japan: A Tendency Towards Formalism—1: The Roots." *Canadian Architect,* vol. 11, no. 12 (December 1966): 28–36.

"Graham House, West Vancouver Island, British Columbia." *Architecture Canada,* vol. 43, no. 12 (December 1966): 44–47.

"Smith House, West Vancouver, British Columbia." *Architecture Canada,* vol. 43, no. 12 (December 1966): 47–50.

"Building and Design." Lecture sponsored by the Department of Extension, University of British Columbia at the Georgia Hotel, Vancouver, March 1967. In the collection of the Canadian Centre for Architecture, Montreal.

"The University: A New Visual Environment." *Canadian Architect,* vol. 13, no. 1 (January 1968): 26–37.

Introduction. *Canadian Architecture, 1960–1970* by Carol M. Ede. Toronto: Burns and McEachern, 1971.

"Address to the Institute of Canadian Bankers." Lecture on October 16, 1972. Arthur Erickson Architect website. www.arthurerickson.com/sp_bankers.html.

Arthur Erickson Architects. *Block 51–61–71: Three-Block Concept.* Mimeograph submission in the office papers of Cornelia Hahn Oberlander, 1973. Partial copy in the collection of the Canadian Centre for Architecture, Montreal.

The Architecture of Arthur Erickson. Montreal: Tundra Books of Montreal, 1975.

"Architecture, Urban Development, and Industrialization." *Canadian Architect,* vol. 20, no. 1 (January 1975): 35–38.

"Sharing—The Choice Is Ours." Address to the American Society of Planning Officials, Vancouver, April 14, 1975. In the collection of the Division of Rare and Manuscript Collections, Cornell University Library.

with J. Lowndes. "Gordon Smith: Three Views." *Artscanada,* no. 208–209 (October/November 1976): 48–50.

"The Design of a House." *Artscanada,* no. 38 (March 1982): 98–101.

New Canadian Chancery: Washington, D.C. Project Proposal, [ca. 1984]. In the collection of the Canadian Centre for Architecture, Montreal.

The Architecture of Arthur Erickson. Text by Allen Steele. Foreword by Peter Blake. Vancouver and Toronto: Douglas & McIntyre, 1988.

"Revitalizing Our Cities." *Plan Canada,* vol. 33, no. 4 (November/December 1993): 47–48.

Introduction. "Contemporary Architects." Edited by Muriel Emanuel. New York: St. Martin's Press, 1994, 289.

"Thoughts on Architecture: A Personal View." Unpublished manuscript, 1999. In the collection of the Canadian Centre for Architecture, Montreal.

"Speech to McGill University School of Architecture." Speech at McGill University, Montreal, October 21, 2000. Arthur Erickson Architect website. www.arthurerickson.com/sp_mcgill.html.

WRITINGS ON ERICKSON AND HIS PROJECTS

Architecture of Arthur Erickson. Vancouver: Vancouver Art Gallery, January 1966.

"Arthur Erickson." *Architectural Digest*, vol. 35, no. 2 (March 1978): 98.

Blake, Peter. Foreword in *The Architecture of Arthur Erickson*. Text by Allen Steele. Vancouver and Toronto: Douglas & McIntyre, 1988.

Boddy, Trevor. "Arthur Erickson's Vancouver Art Gallery." *Section a*, vol. 2, no. 2 (April 1984): 4–21.

———. "Art's Gallery: Original Architect, 1906, Francis Mawson Rattenbury, Architect for Conversion, Arthur Erickson." *Canadian Heritage*, vol. 10, no. 4 (October/November 1981): 30–314.

———. "Erickson in Washington: Canadian Chancery." *Canadian Architect*, vol. 33, no. 1 (January 1988): 12–18.

———. "Erickson's Vancouver: Cityscape 1." *Vancouver Sun*, June 12, 2004.

———. "Landscape of Ideas." *Canadian Architect*, vol. 47, no. 11 (November 2002): 30–36.

———. The Lion in Winter." *Vancouver Sun*, January 26, 2002.

———. "The Design of the University of Lethbridge: Arthur Erickson in His Own Words." *Lethbridge Modern: Aspects of Architectural Modernism in Lethbridge from 1945–1970*. Edited by Gerald Forseth. Lethbridge: Southern Alberta Art Gallery, 2002, 48–53.

"Building in the Doric Tradition: The New MacMillan Bloedel Building." *Architectural Record*, (April 1970): 123–28.

"The Canadian Chancery: A Review." *Urbis* 6 (1989): 11–14.

"The Canadian Pavilion Expo '70, Osaka, Japan." *Canadian Architect*, vol. 15, no. 7 (July 1970): 48–53.

"Canadian Spectacular." *The Architectural Forum* (April 1970): 34–35.

"Casa Graham, West Vancouver, Columbia Britannica." *L'Architettura*, vol. 15, no. 3 (July 1969): 184–85.

Clarkson, Adrienne. *Arthur Erickson*. Interview with Arthur Erickson. Canadian Broadcasting Corporation Archives. n.d.

Ditmars, Hadani. "Built to Last." *Report on Business Magazine*, July 18, 2001, 10.

Ede, Carol M. *Canadian Architecture, 1960–1970*. Introduction by Arthur Erickson, Toronto: Burns and McEachern, 1971.

Franck, Claude. "Lethbridge: A Ship on the Prairie." *L'Architecture d'Aujourd'hui*, no. 183 (January 1976): 46–50.

Freedman, Adele. "Sight Lines: Looking at Architecture and Design in Canada." Toronto: Oxford University Press, 1990.

———. "Modern Art." *Elm Street*, vol. 4, no. 8 (September 2000): 108–12.

———. "Where's the Erickson We Thought We Knew?" *Globe and Mail*, November 4, 1989.

Gill, Alexandra. "Great Panes." *Globe and Mail*, July 16, 2002.

———. "I've Been Very Misunderstood." *Globe and Mail*, February 15, 2001.

Godrey, Stephen. "For Erickson, Home is Where the Work Is." *Globe and Mail*, October 19, 1985.

Goldberger, Paul. "Centerpiece of Vancouver: Gimmick-Free Courthouse." *New York Times*, November 25, 1979.

———. "A New Embassy Mixes the Appropriate and the Awkward." *New York Times*, July 9, 1989.

Hawthorn, Audrey. *A Labour of Love, The Making of the Museum of Anthropology, UBC: The First Three Decades, 1947–1976*. Vancouver: UBC Press, 1993.

"Hotel: Apartment Hotel, Vancouver." *Canadian Architect*, vol. 14, no. 11 (November 1969): 52.

Hynes, Stephen. "Arthur Erickson: Vision for a New Order." *The Social Developer*, Web Organ of Hillside Properties, Vancouver, 2002. www.hillside.ca/1540/erickson.html.

Iglauer, Edith. "Profiles: Seven Stones." *New Yorker,* June 4, 1979, 43–86.

———. *Seven Stones: A Portrait of Arthur Erickson, Architect.* Vancouver: Harbour Publishing and Seattle: University of Washington Press, 1981.

Kalman, Harold. *A History of Canadian Architecture,* vol. II. Toronto: Oxford University Press, 1994.

Koolhaas, Rem and Ian Wakefield. "Arthur Erickson Versus the All-Stars: The Battle of Bunker Hill." *Trace,* vol. 1, no. 3 (July–September 1981): 9–15.

Lownsbrough, John. "At Home with Arthur Erickson." *Western Living,* June 1988, 52–57.

MacKenzie, Colin. "Canada's New Embassy Turns Heads in Washington." *Globe and Mail,* June 29, 1988.

Massey, Erickson. "The University of Lethbridge, Project One." *Architectural Record,* May 1973, 115–24.

———. "Universities: Simon Fraser University, Burnaby, B.C." *Architecture Canada,* vol. 43, no. 10 (October 1966): 43–66.

Margolies, John S. "Twin Towers in Vancouver, B.C., Canada." *Architectural Forum* (April 1970): 42–47.

Mazzariol, Giuseppe. "Il linguaggio di Erickson." *Lotus,* no. 5 (1968): 161–87.

McCabe, Daniel. "A Fine Balance: The Art and Science of Architecture (Part 2)." *McGill News,* vol. 83, no. 2 (Summer 2003): 30–32.

McKenzie, Sandra. "Arthur Erickson." *Canadian House & Home,* vol. 13, no. 1 (February/March 1991): 80–85.

McLaughlin, Michael. "The Communitarian Capitalist." *The Republic,* Vancouver, September 16–19, 2004.

McLennan, Gordon. *The Life and Times of Arthur Erickson.* Videorecording. Vancouver: Dilemma Productions, Moving Images Distribution, 2004. In the collection of the Canadian Centre for Architecture, Montreal.

McMillan, Elizabeth. "Balboa Residence." *Beach Houses: From Malibu to Laguna.* New York: Rizzoli, 1994, 162–67.

McMordie, Michael J. "Contemporary Architects." Edited by Muriel Emanuel. New York: St. Martin's Press, 1994, 289–90.

———. "Modern Architecture." *Canadian Architect,* vol. 29, no. 3 (March 1984): 22.

"The Napp Masterpiece: A Spectacular Symbol of Modern Architecture." *Team Spirit,* house journal of Napp Laboratories (October 1983): 7–10. In the collection of the Canadian Centre for Architecture, Montreal.

Pickering, Edward A. "Building a Concert Hall." Speech on Roy Thomson Hall/Massey Hall to the Rotary Club of Toronto, January 21, 1983. In the collection of the Canadian Centre for Architecture, Montreal.

Polo, Marco-Louis. "Rain Forest Green." *Canadian Architect,* vol. 47, no. 1 (January 2002): 22–23.

"Progress Report: Robson Square, Vancouver." *Canadian Architect,* vol. 24, no. 11 (November 1979): 34–41.

Nairn, Janet. "Vancouver's Grand New Government Center." *Architectural Record* (December 1980): 65–75.

Stephens, Suzanne. "Law Courts/Robson Square, Vancouver." *Progressive Architecture,* March 1981, 82–87.

Rochon, Lisa. "Cityscape: Erickson's Pipe Dream." *Globe and Mail,* June 19, 2002.

———. "Blueprint for Chaos." *Report on Business Magazine,* vol. 6, no. 10 (April 1990): 59–69.

Rogatnick, Abraham. "Simon Fraser University, British Columbia." *The Architectural Review.* vol. 143 (April 1968): 262–75.

Rose, Alison. "Seen and Heard." *Canadian Architect,* vol. 47, no. 11 (November 2002): 20–23.

Rybczynski, Witold. "Visionary in Stone." *The Gazette* (Montreal), December 24, 1988.

Scott, Simon. "The Most Fabulous House in Canada." *architectureBC,* no. 3 (Winter 2001–2002): 16–17.

Shadbolt, Douglas. *Ron Thom: The Shaping of an Architect.* Vancouver: Douglas & McIntyre, 1995.

Shapiro, Barbara. "The Three-Block Project: Classism [*sic*] and Modernism Combined." *West Coast Review,* vol. 15, no. 4 (Spring 1981): 10–18.

Shapiro, Barbara E., and Rhodri Windsor-Liscombe. *Arthur Erickson: Selected Projects 1971–1985*. New York: Centre for Inter-American Relations, 1985.

Schmertz, Mildred F. "Spaces for Anthropological Art, Arthur Erickson's New Museum for the University of British Columbia." *Architectural Record* (May 1977): 103–10.

Smolkin, Michèle. *Arthur Erickson, Concrete Poetry*. Film. Vancouver: Production Radio-Canada Television, 2003.

Thomas, Christopher. "Reconciling the Universal and the Particular: Arthur Erickson in the 1940s and 1950s." *Society for the Study of Architecture in Canada Bulletin*, no. 21 (June 1996): 36–43.

"Three Block, Three Dimensional Park Unifies Old and New Buildings in Downtown Area." *Architectural Record*, vol. 162 (December 1974): 92–93.

Vancouver Art and Artists, 1931–1983. Vancouver: Vancouver Art Gallery, 1983.

"Vancouver Dazzling Center." *Time*, no. 114 (October 1979): 72–74.

Vastokas, Joan M. "Architecture as Cultural Expression: Arthur Erickson and the New Museum of Anthropology, University of British Columbia." *Artscanada*, no. 33 (October/November 1976): 1–15.

Waddell, Gene. *The Design for Simon Fraser University and the Problems Accompanying Excellence*. Unpublished draft manuscript, February 5, 1998. In the collection of the Canadian Centre for Architecture, Montreal.

Windsor-Liscombe, Rhodri. "Erickson Exhibition Reveals the Architect's Design Process." *Canada Today*, no. 11 (April 1986): n.p.

———. Brian Carter and Trevor Boddy. "Arthur Erickson." *World Architecture*, no. 21 (January 1993): 22–43.

ARCHIVAL SOURCES

The following important archives provided access to primary source material for research on Arthur Erickson and his work:

Canadian Centre for Architecture, Montreal
Canadian Architectural Archives, University of Calgary, Canada
John Bland Canadian Architecture Collection,
    McGill University, Montreal
Arthur Erickson Office, Vancouver

The Arthur Erickson Archives

Arthur Erickson has divided the bulk of the archives of his work among three Canadian repositories. The Canadian Architectural Archives of the University of Calgary primarily houses materials produced up to 1974. The Canadian Centre for Architecture principally holds archives of North American work after 1974 as well as conceptual sketches, models and other documents that were retained as artwork by the architect or otherwise excluded from the original transfer to Calgary. The John Bland Canadian Architecture Collection of McGill University holds virtually all documentation of work in the Middle East and the Islamic world and some student projects. Especially for the period from 1972, when the Erickson/Massey partnership was dissolved, to 1976, when the first major transfer to Calgary was made, there may be occasional overlapping of material between the three collections. It is also important to note that much conceptual and development work for early projects, especially domestic ones, may have been discarded and that Erickson's conception of design was often developed through rough-and-ready massing models that have either been destroyed or degraded.

The Canadian Architectural Archives at Calgary counts some 25,000 drawings in its collection; nearly 40 metres of project records, specifications and client and contractor correspondence; and about 300 display panels and photographs. The collection, which consists of more than 200 projects dating from 1948 to 1974, is rich in detail and contains conceptual sketches and design development drawings, as well as working drawings for Erickson's earlier projects that established him as an architect of international importance. Significant works covered include some student work, the design of the Dal Grauer cabana and the Filberg house, the master plan of Simon Fraser University, the Canadian Pavilions at Expo 67 and Osaka 70, the MacMillan Bloedel Building, the University of Lethbridge and the Museum of Anthropology.

The Canadian Centre for Architecture has very extensive holdings of drawings, models and project records from the offices of Arthur Erickson Associates in Vancouver, Toronto and Los Angeles. For work predating 1972, the CCA notably includes the large planning model and competition records for Simon Fraser University, records of public work that remained in the Toronto office, and conceptual sketches selected for the 1988 exhibition of the Americas Society. Beginning with the later stages of design for Robson Square and the Museum of Anthropology in 1974, the drawn record becomes increasingly comprehensive, and both study and presentation models may also be present. There is a notable record of competition submissions, and sketches and conceptual drawings in the architect's hand for more recent work can be extensive. The CCA maintains an ongoing transfer policy with Erickson in which records of new work are regularly added to the collection.

Erickson undertook some forty projects in the Middle East, most of them large-scale public projects and most unbuilt. The presence of the Institute for Islamic Studies at McGill University and the involvement of the School of Architecture with this region provided a critical context for the archive of this work in the Islamic world. Included are some 1500 drawings, created between 1976 and 1986, for over a dozen projects in Saudi Arabia, Iraq, the United Arab Emirates and other countries; more than 100 photographs; records of competition submissions and project development, and four important presentation models: for the Islamic University of Al-Madinah; the redevelopment of the Abu Nuwas area of Baghdad; the Saudi Arabian National Center for Science & Technology science halls; and the headquarters building for Etisalat, the Emirates Telecommunications Corporation.

Among personal records remaining with the architect or his family are travel photographs and correspondence, paintings, prints, handmade greeting and publicity cards, and other materials in which Erickson's visual thinking and observations are significantly represented.

Biographical Notes on the Contributors

NICHOLAS OLSBERG was Director of the Canadian Centre for Architecture from July 2001 to May 2004. Dr. Olsberg joined the CCA as Head of Collections in 1989, when the institution opened, and later served as chief curator from 1990 to 2001. Previously, he was founding head of the Archives of the History of Art at the Getty Center for the History of Art and the Humanities, directed the Master's Program in History and Archival Methods at the University of Massachusetts, was Archivist of the Commonwealth of Massachusetts and was Visiting Fellow in History at Johns Hopkins University. His publications include works on the political and literary culture of the American South, American colonial administration, American architecture in the twentieth century, and archival and museum theory. He holds an honours degree in modern history from Oxford University and a doctorate in American history from the University of South Carolina.

RICARDO L. CASTRO, MRAIC, received the degree of Arquitecto from the Universidad de Los Andes in Bogotá, and an MA in Art History and an M.Arch. from the University of Oregon. He has taught at the Universidad de Los Andes, Bogotá, the University of Oregon, Kansas State University and the University of Laval. He is now an associate professor of Architecture at McGill University, where he has taught since 1982. He was the director of IRHA (Institut de recherche en histoire de l'architecture) from 2000 to 2003. In 1990, Castro was awarded the Prix Paul-Henri Lapointe in the category "History, Criticism and Theory" by the Ordre des architectes du Québec. Castro contributes architectural criticism and photographs to national and international architectural publications, has participated in numerous photographic exhibitions in North America and has contributed to a number of collections of architectural essays. In 1998, he published a book on Colombian architect Rogelio Salmona.

EDWARD DIMENDBERG, an associate professor of Film and Media Studies and Visual Studies at the University of California, Irvine, also has taught at the University of Michigan, the Southern California Institute of Architecture, UCLA and Rice University. He has received fellowships from the Fulbright Commission, the J. Paul Getty Trust, the Graham Foundation, the Canadian Centre for Architecture and the International Research Center for Cultural Sciences in Vienna. He has published widely on film theory and the relation of the mass media to the built environment. Recently, he contributed to the catalogue of a retrospective for works by architects

Diller + Scofidio at the Whitney Museum of American Art and wrote on the redesign of Lincoln Center for the catalogue of the 2004 Architecture Biennial in Venice. Dimendberg is the author of *Excluded Middle: Toward a Reflective Architecture and Urbanism* and *Film Noir and the Spaces of Modernity;* a co-editor (with Anton Kaes and Martin Jay) of *The Weimar Republic Sourcebook* and the *Weimar and Now: German Cultural Criticism* book series. He is working on two books, a study of film and twentieth-century modernization, and *Architecture and the Projected Image.*

LAURENT STALDER has a master's degree in architecture and a doctorate from the Swiss Federal Institute of Technology (ETH Zurich). He is assistant professor at the Institute of History and Theory of Architecture of the Department of Architecture, ETH Zurich. Previously he was assistant professor in the Department of History at the University of Laval in Quebec City, as well as a scholar at the Swiss Institute for Architectural and Archeological Research in Ancient Egypt, Cairo. He has published essays and architectural reviews in a number of journals, as well as co-curating exhibitions, contributing to exhibition catalogues and presenting papers at conferences. He is working on a book, *Wie man ein Haus baut. Hermann Muthesius—Das Landhaus als kulturgeschichtlicher Entwurf,* to be published by GTA Verlag, Zurich, and Ernst & Sohn, Berlin.

GEORGES TEYSSOT has been a professor at the School of Architecture at the University of Laval in Quebec City since 2004. Previously, he was professor of architectural history at the Istituto Universitario di Architettura di Venezia in Italy, and professor of architecture (history and theory) and director of the doctoral program at the School of Architecture, Princeton University. He has published a number of books on architecture, including *Interior Landscapes; The Architecture of Western Gardens: A Design History from the Renaissance to the Present day,* edited with Monique Mosser, republished as *The History of Garden Design: The Western Tradition from the Renaissance to the Present Day,* and edited *The American Lawn: Surface of Everyday Life.*

DAVID THEODORE is a research associate and lecturer in the School of Architecture, and also teaches design in the undergraduate and master's professional programs, at McGill University in Montreal. He is researching the history of healthcare architecture for the project "Medicine by Design," which is directed by Annmarie Adams and funded by the Canadian Institutes of Health Research. He has published on diverse topics including the architecture of Ludwig Wittgenstein and a history of the children's hospital in Canada (with A. Adams). He regularly reviews architecture and design for publications including *Architecture, Azure, Canadian Architect* and *Maisonneuve.*

Image Credits

CAA: Canadian Architectural Archives, University of Calgary, Arthur Erickson fond
CCA: Arthur Erickson Archive, Collection Centre Canadien d'Architecture/Canadian Centre for Architecture, Montreal

5 Photo © Ricardo L. Castro, 2005.
6 Courtesy of Geoff Erickson.
9 Photo by Simon Scott.
17 Photo by Simon Scott.
18 Photo by Simon Scott.
21 top: © Arthur Erickson.
21 bottom left: Photo by Dick Busher, Cosgrove Editions, Seattle, 791116-26.
21 bottom right: © Arthur Erickson.
22 top left: Photo by Simon Scott.
22 top right: © Arthur Erickson.
22 bottom left: © Arthur Erickson.
22 bottom right: © Arthur Erickson.
23 top: © Arthur Erickson.
23 bottom: Photo by Simon Scott.
24 © Arthur Erickson.
25 top: *Sketch, partial east section, Museum of Anthropology, University of British Columbia, Vancouver, British Columbia,* c. 1971, ink and graphite on tracing paper, 34.0 × 93.0cm, 022 ARC 053, CCA.
25 bottom: *Sketch, plan, ramped and massive galleries, Museum of Anthropology, University of British Columbia, Vancouver, British Columbia,* c. 1971, ink and colour pencil on tracing paper, 78.7 × 53.3cm (irregular), 022 ARC 052, CCA.
26 top: © Arthur Erickson.
26 bottom left: *Conceptual notations, Private Residence, Pacific North-West (also called "Bagley Wright House"),* c. 1977, photomechanical print, 21.5 × 27.9cm, 022 ARC 021, CCA.
26 bottom centre: *Conceptual sketch, site plan with house, Private residence, Pacific North-west (also called "Bagley Wright House"),* c. 1977, photomechanical transfer, 21.5 × 27.9cm, 022 ARC 022, CCA.
26 bottom right: *Sketch, plan, Private Residence, Pacific North-west (also called "Bagley Wright House"),* c. 1977, photomechanical transfer, 21.5 × 27.9cm, 022 ARC 024, CCA.

27 all: *Advanced study model, Private Residence, Pacific North-West (also called "Bagley Wright House"),* c. 1977, Styrofoam, paper and foamcore, 17.8 × 198.1 × 88.9cm, 022 ARC 184, CCA.
29 top: © Arthur Erickson.
29 bottom: *Sketches, interior perspective with elevation and section details, Private Residence, Pacific North-West (also called "Bagley Wright House"),* c. 1977, photomechanical transfer, 21.5 × 27.9cm, 022 ARC 025, CCA.
30 top: *Study model, Puget Sound House, Washington State,* 1983, foamcore, paper, cardboard and sponge, 30.5 × 60.7 × 74.9cm, 022 ARC 187 A, CCA.
30 bottom left: *Study model, Puget Sound House, Washington State,* 1983, foamcore, wood and cardboard, 20.3 × 87.6 × 95.2cm, 022 ARC 186 D, CCA.
30 bottom right: *Study model, Puget Sound House, Washington State,* 1983, foamcore, wood, acrylic and paper, 22.9 × 153.7 × 100.3cm, 022 ARC 188 D, CCA.
31 Photo © Russell Abraham, 2005.
32 Photo by Tim Street-Porter.
60 top: From "A Tendency towards Formalism: The Roots," *Canadian Architect* 11 (December 1966): 32–33. Reproduced courtesy of *Canadian Architect.*
60 bottom: From "The Weight of Heaven," *Canadian Architect* 9 (March 1964): 52–53. Reproduced courtesy of *Canadian Architect.*
63 From *Habitation: Space, Dilemma and Design,* Ottawa: Canadian Housing Design Council, 1965. Photo by Trevor Mills, Vancouver Art Gallery.
72 all: Courtesy of CAA.
73 all: Courtesy of CAA.
74 all: Courtesy of CAA.
75 top: Courtesy of CAA.
75 bottom: © Arthur Erickson.
76 all: Courtesy of CAA.
79 all: Photo © Ricardo L. Castro, 2005.
80 top left: Photo by Michael Manni/Napp Laboratories, 1982.
80 top right: Sketches, perspective and plan, NAPP Laboratories, Cambridge, England, c. 1979, ink on tracing paper, 21.5 × 30.5cm (irregular), 022 ARC 185, CCA.
80 bottom: © Arthur Erickson.
81 top: Photo by Trevor Mills, Vancouver Art Gallery.
81 bottom: Courtesy of Nick Milkovich Architects, Inc.
82 all: Courtesy of Nick Milkovich Architects, Inc.
113 top: Courtesy of CAA.

113 bottom: Photo courtesy of IBM.
114 Photo © Wayne Andrews/Esto. All rights reserved.
117 top: Photo by Stewarts Commercial Photographers & Finishers, courtesy of Skidmore, Owings & Merrill LLP (SOM).
117 bottom: Photo courtesy of Moshe Safdie and Associates.
118 left: Photo © Ezra Stoller/Esto. All rights reserved.
118 right: Photo by Manfred Schiedelm.
120 Photo by Nick Wheeler, courtesy of The Architects Collaborative (TAC).
121 Courtesy of CAA.
122 Photo by Jean-Claude Planchet/G. Meguerditchian. Courtesy CNAC/MNAM/Dist. Réunion des Musées Nationaux/Art Resource, New York.
130 © Arthur Erickson.
131 top left: Photo © Ezra Stoller/Esto. All rights reserved.
131 top right: Courtesy of CAA.
131 bottom: Courtesy of CAA.
132 all: Courtesy of CAA.
135 top: Photo by Simon Scott.
135 bottom: Photo by Frank Mayrs.
136 *Aerial view of the site, Robson Square, Vancouver, British Columbia,* June 26, 1973, gelatin silver print, 50.2 × 40.5cm, 022 ARC 194, CCA.
137 top left: *Presentation drawing, east-west section, Robson Square, Three Block Project, Vancouver, British Columbia,* after 1973, photomechanical transfer, 21.5 × 27.8cm, 022 ARC 191, CCA.
137 top right: *Presentation drawing, east-west section, Law Courts, Three Block Project, Vancouver, British Columbia,* after 1973, photomechanical transfer, 27.8 × 20.7cm, 022 ARC 190, CCA.
137 bottom: *Presentation model, original concept, Three Block Project, Vancouver, British Columbia,* c. 1973, wood and plastic, 16.5 × 137.2 × 43.2cm, 022 ARC 076, CCA.
138 top: Photo by Simon Scott.
138 bottom: Photo courtesy of Arthur Erickson.
139 © Arthur Erickson.
140 Photo © Mark Darley/Esto. All rights reserved.
141 top left: *Preliminary study models, Canadian Chancery, Washington, D.C.,* 1982, Styrofoam, 10.2 × 19.0 × 12.7cm (each), 022 ARC 114, CCA.
141 top right: *Sketch, elevation, J. Marshall Park, Canadian Chancery, Washington, D.C.,* 1982, ink on tracing paper, 35.6 × 58.4cm, 022 ARC 189, CCA.
141 bottom: © Arthur Erickson.
142 all: Courtesy of Nick Milkovich Architects, Inc.
143 all: Photo by Trevor Mills, Vancouver Art Gallery.
176 Photo by Wilson Duff, courtesy of the British Columbia Archives, Royal British Columbia Museum Corporation, Victoria.
178 Photo by Jim Banham, courtesy of the University of British Columbia Archives.
179 Photo by Philip Doyle for Vancouver Art Gallery.

All portfolio photographs © Ricardo L. Castro.

Index of Works Cited